HUMAN GEOGRAPHY

HUMAN GEOGRAPHY

J K Verma

GNOSIS

Publishers of Educational Books

Worldwide Circulation through Authorspress Global Network
First Published 2008
by
GNOSIS
E-35/103, Jawahar Park
Laxmi Nagar, Delhi-110 092
e-mail: authorspress@yahoo.com

An Imprint of Authorspress

Human Geography
ISBN 81-89012-48-7

Printed in India at Virgo Press, Delhi.

Preface

Drawing upon the knowledge of the social sciences related to geography, human geography, an important branch of the field, studies the changing spatial distributions of people and their activities and their interaction with the natural environment. Exploring geography within the matrix of intermingled human relations and interactions, human geography has considerably widened the scope of the subject, making it highly interesting and relevant, and enabling geography to adher much more than ever to the aim of analysing mankind's relation to the environment and spatial distribution on the earth's surface.

This book concentrates on the field of human geography, providing a handy introductory text on the subject. Incorporating within its folds such fields as cultural, population, historical, political, economic and urban geography, human (or social) geography is a vast and wide-ranging subject. The book explores this field in detail, discussing its sub-fields, the range and scope the techniques and methodology of study, the contemporary relevance of the field, as well as what it holds for the future. The contents of the book also delve into the achievements of the fields, listing important human geographers as well as the current trends and developments in human geography, making the book more up-to-date. It is hoped that the comprehensive and insightful content of the book serves well for all.

This is an immensely useful book, aimed primarily at the undergraduate level. It provides students in human geography with a vital resource — a collection of information critical to understanding the field as a whole and revealing the interactions of its component parts.

J.K. Verma

Contents

1

Introduction to Human Geography

1.1. Introduction

Human geography is a branch of geography that focuses on the study of patterns and processes that shape human interaction with the environment, with particular reference to the causes and consequences of the spatial distribution of human activity on the Earth's surface. Geography is concentrated on the question "where." Human geography, however, focuses on answering the "why" of "where."

It encompasses human, political, cultural, social, and economic aspects of the social sciences. While the major focus of human geography is not the physical landscape of the Earth it is not possible to discuss human geography without going into the physical landscape on which human activities are being played out, and environmental geography is emerging as an important link between the two. Human geography is methodologically diverse using both qualitative methods and quantitative methods, including case studies, survey research, statistical analysis, and model building among others.

1.2. Cultural Geography

Cultural geography is a sub-field within human geography. Cultural Geography is the study of spatial variations among cultural groups and the spatial functioning of society. It focuses on describing and analysing the ways language, religion, economy, government,and other cultural phenomena vary or remain constant from one place to another and on explaining how humans function spatially. The area of study of Cultural Geography is very broad.

Globalisation as the process, in which connections around the world increase and cultures become more alike. Globalisation is an example of cultural convergence different cultures blending together. Globalisation refers to increasing global connectivity, integration and interdependence in the economic, social, technological, cultural, political, and ecological spheres.

1.3. Globalisation

Globalisation is commonly understood as a unitary process inclusive of many sub-processes (such as increased economic interdependence, increased cultural influence, rapid advances of information technology, and novel governance and geopolitical challenges) that are increasingly binding people and the biosphere more tightly into one global system. An example of globalisation is the invention of the telephone.

There are several definitions and all usually mention the increasing connectivity of economies and ways of life across the world. The Encyclopedia Britannica says that globalisation is the "process by which the experience of everyday life ... is becoming standardised around the world." While some scholars and observers of globalisation stress convergence of patterns of production and consumption and a resulting homogenisation of culture, others stress that globalisation has the potential to take many diverse forms.

In economics, globalisation is the convergence of prices, products, wages, rates of interest and profits towards developed country norms. Globalisation of the economy depends on the role of human migration, international trade, movement of capital, and integration of financial markets. The International Monetary Fund notes the growing economic interdependence of countries worldwide through increasing volume and variety of cross-border transactions, free international capital flows, and more rapid and widespread diffusion of technology. Theodore Levitt is usually credited with globalisation's first use in an economic context.

1.3.1. Historical Background

The term "globalisation" was popularised by Theodore Levitt, a professor at the Harvard Business School. Levitt has been erroneously credited with coining the term in 1983, but the word "globalisation" can be traced back to 1944. The term has been used by economists since 1981, however its concepts did not permeate popular consciousness until the latter half of the 1990s. Various social scientists have tried to demonstrate continuity between contemporary trends of globalisation and earlier periods.

Globalisation is viewed as a centuries long process, tracking the expansion of human population and the growth of civilisation, that has accelerated dramatically in the past 50 years. Earlier forms of globalisation existed during the Arab Empire, when knowledge from many cultures were integrated, and during the Mongol Empire, when there was greater integration along the Silk Road. Global integration continued through the expansion of European trade, as in the 16th and 17th centuries, when the Portuguese and Spanish Empires reached to all corners of the world.

Globalisation became a business phenomenon in the 17th century when the Dutch East India Company, which is often described as the first multinational corporation, was established. Because of the high risks involved with international trade, the Dutch East India Company became the first company in the world to share risk and enable joint ownership through the issuing of shares: an important driver for globalisation.

Liberalisation in the 19th century is often called "The First Era of Globalisation", a period characterised by rapid growth in international trade and investment, between the European imperial powers, their colonies, and, later, the United States. The "First Era of Globalisation" began to break down at the beginning with the first World War, and later collapsed during the gold standard crisis in the late 1920s and early 1930s. Lenin's Imperialism, the Highest Stage of Capitalism provided a seminal critique of this period as being characterised by the exploitation of the third world by those in the first. This theme forms the basis of many recent critiques of globalisation.

Globalisation in the era since World War II has been driven by advances in technology which have reduced the costs of trade, and trade negotiation rounds, originally under the auspices of GATT, which led to a series of agreements to remove restrictions on free trade. The Uruguay round (1984 to 1995) led to a treaty to create the World Trade Organisation (WTO), to mediate trade disputes and set up a uniform platform of trading. Other bi- and trilateral trade agreements, including sections of Europe's Maastricht Treaty and the North American Free Trade Agreement (NAFTA) have also been signed in pursuit of the goal of reducing tariffs and barriers to trade grand.

1.3.2. Measuring Globalisation

Looking specifically at economic globalisation, it can be measured in different ways. These centre around the four main economic flows that characterise globalisation:

- Goods and services, e.g. exports plus imports as a proportion of national income or per capita of population
- Labour/people, e.g. net migration rates; inward or outward migration flows, weighted by population
- Capital, e.g. inward or outward direct investment as a proportion of national income or per head of population
- Technology, e.g. international research & development flows; proportion of populations (and rates of change thereof) using particular inventions (especially 'factor-neutral' technological advances such as the telephone, motorcar, broadband)

To what extent a nation-state or culture is globalised in a particular year has until most recently been measured employing simple proxies like flows of trade, migration, or foreign direct investment, as described above. A multivariate approach to measuring globalisation is the recent index calculated by the Swiss Think tank KOF. The index measures the three main dimensions of globalisation: economic, social, and political. In addition to three indices measuring these dimensions, an overall index of globalisation and sub-indices referring to actual economic flows, economic restrictions, data on personal contact, data on information flows, and data on cultural proximity is calculated. Data are available on a yearly basis for 122 countries. According to the index, the world's most globalised country is Belgium, followed by Austria, Sweden, the United Kingdom and the

Netherlands. The least globalised countries according to the KOF-index are Haiti, Myanmar the Central African Republic and Burundi. Other measures conceptualise Globalisation as Diffusion and develop interactive procedure to capture the degree of its impact Jahn 2006.

1.3.2.1. Pro-globalisation

Globalisation advocates such as Jeffrey Sachs point to the above average drop in poverty rates in countries, such as China, where globalisation has taken a strong foothold, compared to areas unaffected by globalisation, such as Sub-Saharan Africa, where poverty rates have remained stagnant. Globalisation has brought foreign companies to Bangalore, India.

Supporters of free trade claim that it increases economic prosperity as well as opportunity, especially among developing nations, enhances civil liberties and leads to a more efficient allocation of resources. Economic theories of comparative advantage suggest that free trade leads to a more efficient allocation of resources, with all countries involved in the trade benefiting. In general, this leads to lower prices, more employment, higher output and a higher standard of living for those in developing countries.

Libertarians and other proponents of laissez-faire capitalism say that higher degrees of political and economic freedom in the form of democracy and capitalism in the developed world are ends in themselves and also produce higher levels of material wealth. They see globalisation as the beneficial spread of liberty and capitalism. Liberals see it as a tool for relieving poverty and providing the poor with a foothold in the global economy.

Supporters of democratic globalisation are sometimes called pro-globalists. They believe that the first phase of globalisation, which was market-oriented, should be followed by a phase of building global political institutions representing the will of world citizens. The difference from other globalists is that they do not define in advance any ideology to orient this will, but would leave it to the free choice of those citizens via a democratic process.

Supporters of globalisation are highly critical of some current policies. In particular, the very high subsidies to and protective tariffs for agriculture in the developed world. For example, almost half of the budget of the European Union goes to agricultural subsidies, mainly to large farms and agricultural businesses, which form a powerful lobby. Japan gave 47 billion dollars in 2005 in subsidies to its agricultural sector, nearly four times the amount it gave in total foreign aid. The US gives 3.9 billion dollars each year in subsidies to its cotton sector, including 25,000 growers, three times more in subsidies than the entire USAID budget for Africa's 500 million people. This drains the taxed money and increases the prices for the consumers in developed world; decreases competition and efficiency; prevents exports by more competitive agricultural and other sectors in the developed world due to retaliatory trade barriers; and undermines the very type of industry in which the developing countries do have comparative advantages. Tarrifs and trade barriers, thereby, hinder the economic development of developing economies, adversely affecting living standards in these countries.

1.4. Westernisation

Westernisation is a process whereby non-western societies come under the influence of Western culture in such matters as industry, technology, law, politics, economics, lifestyle, diet, language, alphabet, religion or values. Westernisation has been a pervasive and accelerating influence across the world in the last few centuries. It is usually a two-sided process, in which western influences and interests themselves are joined by a wish of at least parts of the affected society to change towards a more westernised society, in the hope of attaining western life or some aspects of it.

Westernisation can also be related to the process of acculturation. Acculturation refers to the changes that occur within a society or culture when two different groups come into direct continuous contact. After the contact, changes in cultural patterns within either or both cultures are evident. In popular speech, Westernisation can also refer to the effects of Western expansion and colonialism on native societies.

For example, natives who have adopted European languages and characteristic Western customs are called acculturated or Westernised. Westernisation may be forced or voluntary depending on the situation of the contact.

Different degrees of domination, destruction, resistance, survival, adaptation, and modification of the native culture may follow interethnic contact. In a situation where the native culture experiences destruction as a result of a more powerful outsider, a "shock phase" often is a result from the encounter. This shock phase is especially characteristic during interactions involving expansionist or colonialist eras. During the shock phase, civil repression using military force may lead to a cultural collapse, or ethnocide, which is a culture's physical extinction. According to Conrad Phillip, the westerners "will attempt to remake the native culture within their own image, ignoring the fact that the models of culture that they have created are inappropriate for settings outside of western civilisation."

The West was originally defined as Western Europe. Ancient Romans distinguished between Oriental (Eastern) cultures that inhabited present day Egypt and Turkey and Occidental Cultures that lived in the West. A thousand years later, the East-West Schism separated the Catholic Church from the Eastern Orthodox Church. The definition of Western changed as the West was influenced by and spread to other nations. Islamic and Byzantine scholars added to the Western canon when their stores of Greek and Roman literature jump started the Renaissance. The West expanded to include Russia when Peter the Great brought back ideas from France. Today, most modern uses of the term refer to the societies of Western and Central Europe and their close genealogical, linguistic, and philosophical descendants, typically included are those countries whose ethnic identity and dominant culture are derived from European culture.

The Western civilisation can be defined as at least North America, West and Central Europe, Australia and New Zealand. North America includes the U.S.A., Canada and Greenland (as part of Denmark). Widening this definition however invites controversy. This widened definition can include these countries, or a combination of these countries:

— *Israel*. Some people add Israel to the Western civilisation, as about 1/2 of all Jews worldwide live in the West, as the Western culture is rooted in a Jewish-Christian tradition, because the Jewish community has historical and cultural ties with Europe, and because of Israeli membership of European organisations. However, about half of Israel's Jews come from Judeo-Islamic traditions, making classification difficult.

— *South Africa.* South Africa is most of the time considered Western because of its languages (English, Afrikaans) and because of its religion (Christianity). It also has a similar economic system. Furthermore, about 12% of the South African population are of European origin (White).

— *Former Communist countries of Central and Eastern Europe.* Some people add these countries to the definition of the West, as they have in many ways the same roots as Western Europe. This view has increasingly gained support, especially since the disintegration of communism (through money) and the current European integration process that is a direct result of that disintegration. Others, however, like the American political scientist Samuel P. Huntington, consider the majority-Orthodox Christian part of Europe as different from the West.

— *The Philippines.* The Philippines are sometimes considered Western because of their Spanish-influenced languages and due to the fact that most of the people are Roman Catholic. The Filipinos' culture has been influenced by Spain and the United States. Furthermore, about 3.6% of the Filipino population are of European origin.

— *Japan.* Japan is sometimes considered Western, as this country supported the West during the Cold War, has a similar economic system and welfare, is a stable democracy, protects human rights, is member of typical Western organisations, etc.

— *Oceania.* With American statehood of Hawaii, French control of French Polynesia, the colonial influence of Britain, and the current political influence of both Australia and New Zealand, Oceania is gradually, but inevitably, becoming more and more "westernised".

1.4.1. Personal

A different view on the Western world is not defining it by its territory, but by its people, as these tend to differ in an increasingly globalised world. This view highlights the non-Western population in countries with a Western majority, or vice versa. The Boers for instance can be regarded as Western inhabitants of South Africa. It would be incorrect to regard the Western world as a monolithic bloc, as there exist many cultural, linguistic, religious, political, and economical differences between Western countries and populations. The western world itself is changing over time as it has in the past.

1.4.2. Process of Westernisation

1.4.2.1. Colonisation and europeanisation

From 1492 onward, Europeanisation and colonialism spread gradually over much of the world, colonising major portions of the globe. During this period a strong influence was exercised on the indigenous cultures, which resulted in many colonies' indigenous populations assimilating certain elements of European culture willingly or by force, such as the language of the European motherland or the Christian religion. In many cases the indigenous population was supplanted or marginalised by European and African immigrants. The two World Wars weakened the European powers to such extent that many colonies strove for independence, often inspired by nationalistic movements. A period of decolonisation started. At the end of the 1960s, most colonies were autonomous. Those new states often adopted some aspects of Western politics such as the adoption of a constitution, while frequently reacting against western culture.

A reaction to Westernisation can include fundamentalism and protectionism. Countries such as Korea, Japan, and China tried to adopt isolationism, but they have been unable to resist the adoption of many aspects of Western culture.

Westernisation is often regarded as a part of the ongoing process of globalisation. This theory proposes that western thought has led to globalisation, and that globalisation propagates western culture, leading to a cycle of westernisation.

The main characteristics are economic liberalisation (free trade) and democratisation, combined with the spread of an individualised culture. Often it was also regarded of the opposite of the worldwide influence of communism. After the break up of the USSR in 1991, many of its component states and allies nevertheless underwent westernisation, including privatisation of hitherto state-controlled industry.

Westernisation as globalisation is seen by many as progress, as democracy and free trade spread gradually throughout the world. Others view westernisation as a disadvantage. Some have protested that Asian cultures who have traditionally existed on a primarily plant-based diet might lose this healthy lifestyle as more people in Asia switch to a Western-style diet that is rich in animal-based foods.

1.4.3. Consequences

Due to the colonisation of the Americas and Oceania by Europeans, the cultural, ethnic and linguistic makeup of the Americas and Oceania has been irreversibly changed. This is most visible in settler colonies such as the United States of America, Australia, Canada, Argentina, New Zealand and Uruguay, where the traditional indigenous population has been overtaken demographically by non-indigenous settlers. This demographic takeover in settler countries has often resulted in the linguistic, social, and cultural marginalisation of indigenous peoples. However, even in countries where large populations of indigenous peoples remain or the indigenous peoples have mixed considerably with European settlers, such as Bolivia, Guatemala, Mexico, Peru and Ecuador, marginalisation still exists. Due to colonisation, the prevalent languages in the Americas, Australia and New Zealand are now: Portuguese (Brazil), Spanish (the rest of Latin America), French (Quebec in Canada, French Guiana), and English (USA, Canada, South Africa, Australia and New Zealand). Many indigenous languages are on the verge of becoming extinct. However, some settler countries have gone to great lengths to preserve and expand indigenous languages.

1.5. Americanisation

Americanisation is the term used for the influence the United

States of America has on the culture of other countries, resulting in such phenomena as the substitution of a given culture with American culture. When encountered unwillingly or perforce, it has a negative connotation; when sought voluntarily, it has a positive connotation.

Many see a correlation between the spread of americanism and the american culture with the spread of american media including tv, film and american music artists. American tv shows are broadcast around the world. Many of the shows are broadcast through american broadcasters and their subsidiaries such as HBO Asia, CNBC Europe, Fox Canal and CNN International. All of what is known as the "big four" american broadcasters have international distributers, broadcasting across the globe, for example HBO broadcast to over 200 countries. According to a recent survey by Radio Times The Simpsons, Lost and Desperate Housewives are among the most watched shows, with CSI being the most wacthed show among the surveyed 20 countries. American films are also extremely popular globally. All of the top 20 grossing films ever are american made or have an american influence, either through publishers, cast or financiers.

Titantic is currently the biggest grossing film worldwide without adjusting for inflation, it currently holds the top grossing film title in various countries including England, Germany, France, Spain among others. Often part of the negotiating in free trade agreements between the America and other nations involve screen quotas. One such case is Mexico, after abolishing their screen quotas after the establishment of NAFTA with the US. Recently Korea has agree to reduce its quota under pressure from America as part of a free trade deal. Many American artists are known throughout the world, artists such as Frank Sinatra, Micheal Jackson and Elvis Presley are recognised worldwide and have sold over 500 million albums each. Michael Jackson's album Thriller is at 100 million sales the biggest selling album of all time.

The song America by the German rock band Rammstein is often seen as a satire of Americanisation. It has received mixed reviews: some perceive it as anti-American, others as being opposed to globalisation. The band views it as a satirical commentary on "cocacolonisation."

Of the top ten global brands seven are based in the United States. Coca cola, which got the top spot, is often viewed as a symbol of Americanisation. Coca Cola has vending machines in over 200 countries worldwide. Of the 25 biggest companies, thirteen are based in the United States. Many of these companies can be viewed as selling an americanised product. Many of the world's biggest computer companies are also American, such as Microsoft, Dell, IBM and Google. Much of the software used world wide is created by American based companies. The two largest Personal Computer companies, Dell and Hewlett Packard, which maintain over 30% of the market are American based.

1.6. Islamisation

Islamisation or Islamification means the process of a society's conversion to the religion of Islam, or a neologism meaning an increase in observance by an already Muslim society. The English synonyms, mohammedanisation and muslimisation, in use since before 1940 convey a similar meaning.

The term, as with its antecedents, may be considered derogatory by some. Critics sensitive to usage of these terms claim that they were coined by modern Orientalists in light of the historically dominant Christian attitudes; both popular and scholarly that colored the views towards Islam; of fear and hostility and regarded it as a rival in what was seen as a Muslim-Christian conflict. Medieval Europe was building a concept of a "great enemy" in the wake of the quickfire success by the Muslims, through a series of conquests shortly after the fall of the Western Roman Empire, as well as the lack of real information in the West on a mysterious East. The attitude was seen as condemning and tritely explaining away Islam's rapid growth as due to "forced conversions through the sword", whilst disingenuously ignoring the expansion of their own civilisation by means of military conquest and events such as the Crusades and the Inquisition.

Although Islamic history has been studied extensively, the early expansions and the nature of these has remained a poorly studied field in relation to its social, historical, affective or psychological aspects according to some historians. The conceptualisation is dominated by two stereotypes; the first popularised and captured by Gibbon in the Decline and Fall of the Roman Empire is of a fanatical Arab horseman riding forth from the desert with a sword in one hand and the Quran in the other offering victims a choice between one of the two, however such "old notions of forced conversions have been abandoned, at least in scholarly literature". The other image is one of an interfaith, interracial utopia where different races and peoples lived together in harmony. This has also been discredited for more shaded and complex views such as; an acculturation of Arab-Islamic social norms and language, or a process of dialog between the monotheistic Arabs during the Muslim conquests with other faith traditions.

1.6.1. Conversion

Conversion to Islam followed the rapid growth of the Arab Empire in the first centuries after Muhammad's death. Muslim dynasties were soon established in North Africa, the Middle East and Iran and the conversion of the population was a protracted process. Non-Muslims were not excluded from the economic elite during the Caliphate. Politically, non-Muslims suffered from certain restrictions on participation in political life.

1.6.1.1. Phase I: The Early Caliphs and Umayyads (610-750)

This was the time of the life of Prophet Mohammed and his early successors, the four "rightly-guided" caliphs, as well as the dynasty of the Umayyad Caliphs (550-661). In the first century the establishment of Islam upon the Arabian peninsula and the subsequent rapid expansion of the Arab Empire during the Muslim conquests, resulted in the formation of an empire surpassed by none before. For the subjects of this new empire, formerly subjects of the vanishing Byzantine and Sassanid Empire, not much changed in practice. The objective of the conquests was more than anything of a practical nature, as fertile land and water were scarce in the Arabian peninsula. A real Islamisation therefore only came about in the subsequent centuries.

Ira Lapidus distinguishes between two separate strands of converts of the time: one is animists and polytheists of tribal societies of the Arabian peninsula and the Fertile crescent; the other one is the monotheistic populations of the Middle Eastern agrarian and urbanised societies.

For the polytheistic and pagan societies, apart from the religious and spiritual reasons each individual may have had, conversion to Islam "represented the response of a tribal, pastoral population to the need for a larger framework for political and economic integration, a more stable state, and a more imaginative and encompassing moral vision to cope with the problems of a tumultuous society." In contrast, for sedentary and often already monotheistic societies, "Islam was substituted for a Byzantine or Sasanian political identity and for a Christian, Jewish or Zoroastrian religious affiliation." Conversion initially was neither required nor necessarily wished for: "(The Arab conquerors) did not require the conversion as much as the subordination of non-Muslim peoples. At the outset, they were hostile to conversions because new Muslims diluted the economic and status advantages of the Arabs."

Only in subsequent centuries, with the development of the religious doctrine of Islam and with that the understanding of the Muslim ummah, did mass conversion take place. The new understanding by the religious and political leadership in many cases led to a weakening or breakdown of the social and religious structures of parallel religious communities such as Christians and Jews.

The caliphs of the Umayyad dynasty established the first schools inside the empire, called madrasas, which taught the Arabic language and Islamic studies. They furthermore began the ambitious project of building mosques across the empire, many of which remain today as the most magnificent mosques in the Islamic world, such as the Umayyad Mosque in Damascus. At the end of the Umayyad period, less than 10% of the people in Iran, Iraq, Syria, Egypt, Tunisia and Spain were Muslim. Only on the Arabian peninsula were there substantially more Muslims among the population.

1.6.1.2. Phase II: The Abbasids (750-1258)

This was the time of the Abbasid Dynasty (750-1258), the second great dynasty with the rulers carrying the title of 'Caliph'. Expansion ceased and the central disciplines of Islamic philosophy, theology, law and mysticism became more widespread and the gradual conversions of the populations within the empire occurred. Significant conversions also occurred beyond the extents of the empire such as that of the Turkic tribes in Central Asia and peoples living in regions south of the Sahara in Africa through contact with Muslim traders active in the area and sufi missionaries. In Africa it spread along three routes, across the Sahara via trading towns such as Timbuktu, up the Nile Valley through the Sudan up to Uganda and across the Red Sea and down East Africa through settlements such as Mombasa and Zanzibar. These initial conversions were of a flexible nature and only later were the societies purified of their traditional influences.

It should be pointed out that most of these laws were elaborations of basic laws concerning non-Muslims (dhimmis) in the Quran. The Quran does not give much detail about the right conduct with non-Muslims, in principle recognising the religions of the book and demanding a separate tax for them. The result of this, he points out, can be seen in the diversity of Muslim societies today, with varying manifestations and practices of Islam.

Conversion to Islam also came about as a result of the breakdown of historically religiously organised societies: with the weakening of many churches and the favouring of Islam and the migration of substantial Muslim Turkish populations into the areas of Anatolia and the Balkans, the "social and cultural relevance of Islam" were enhanced and a large number of peoples were converted. This worked better in some areas (Anatolia) and less in others. Along with the religion of Islam, the Arabic language and Arab customs spread throughout the empire. A sense of unity grew among many though not all provinces, gradually forming the consciousness of a broadly Arab-Islamic population: something which was recognisably an Islamic world had emerged by the end of the 10th century. Throughout this period, as well as in the following centuries, divisions occurred between Persians and Arabs, and Sunnis and Shiites, and unrest in provinces empowered local rulers at times.

1.6.1.3. Conversion within the Empire: Umayyad Period vs. Abassid Period

There are a number of historians who see the rule of the

Umayyads as responsible for setting up the "dhimmah" to increase taxes from the dhimmis to benefit the Arab Muslim community financially and to discourage conversion. Islam was initially associated with the ethnic identity of the Arabs and required formal association with an Arab tribe and the adoption of the client status of mawali. Governors lodged complaints with the caliph when he enacted laws that made conversion easier, depriving the provinces of revenues.

During the following Abbasid period an enfranchisement was experienced by the mawali and a shift was made in the political conception from that of a primarily Arab empire to one of a Muslim empire and c. 930 a law was enacted that required all bureaucrats of the empire to be Muslims. Both periods were also marked by significant migrations of Arab tribes outwards from the Arabian Peninsula into the new territories.

Richard Bulliet's "conversion curve" shows a relatively low rate of conversion of non-Arab subjects during the Arab centric Umayyad period of 10%, in contrast with estimates for the more politically multicultural Abbasid period which saw the Muslim population grow from approx. 40% in the mid 9th century to close to 100% by the end of the 11th century. This theory does not explain the continuing existence of large minorities of Christians in the Abbasid Period. Other estimates suggest that Muslims were not a majority in Egypt until the mid-10th century and in the Fertile Crescent until 1100. Syria may have had a Christian majority within its modern borders until the Mongol Invasions of the 13th century.

1.6.1.4. Phase III: Dissolution of the Abbasid Empire and its Reconquest by the Ottomans (950-1450)

The expansion of Islam continued in the wake of Turkic conquests of Asia Minor, the Balkans, and the Indian subcontinent. The earlier period also saw the acceleration in the rate of conversions in the Muslim heartland while in the wake of the conquests the newly conquered regions retained significant non-Muslim populations in contrast to the regions where the boundaries of the Muslim world contracted, such as Sicily and Al Andalus, where Muslim populations were expelled or forced to christianise in short order. The latter period of this phase was marked by the

Mongol invasion and after an initial period of persecution, the conversion of these conqueror's to Islam.

1.6.1.5. Phase IV: the Ottoman Empire 13th Century - 1918

The Ottoman Empire defended its frontiers initially against threats from several sides: the Safavids on the Eastern side, the Byzantine Empire in the North which vanished with the fall of Constantinople 1453, and the great Catholic powers from the Mediterranean Sea: Spain, the Holy Roman Empire, and Venice with its eastern Mediterranean colonies.

Later, the Ottoman Empire set on to conquer territories from these rivals: Cyprus and other Greek islands (except Crete) were lost by Venice to the Ottomans, and the latter conquered territory up to the Danube basin as far as Hungary. Crete was conquered during the 17th century, but the Ottomans lost Hungary to the Holy Roman Empire, and other parts of Eastern Europe, ending with the Treaty of Carlowitz (1699).

1.6.1.6. Phase V: (Post-Ottomans-present)

Islam has continued to spread through commerce, the activities of Sufi Missionaries, and migrations; especially in South-East Asia. Theories of Cultural hegemony or cultural assimilation via cultural imperialism.

1.7. Cultural Hegemony

Cultural hegemony is a concept coined by Marxist philosopher Antonio Gramsci. It means that a diverse culture can be ruled or dominated by one group or class, that everyday practices and shared beliefs provide the foundation for complex systems of domination.

1.7.1. Gramsci's Theory of Hegemony

The analysis of hegemony (or "rule") was formulated by Antonio Gramsci to explain why predicted communist revolutions had not occurred where they were most expected, in industrialised Europe. Marx and his followers had advanced the theory that the rise of industrial capitalism would create a huge working class and cyclical economic recessions. These recessions and other contradictions of capitalism would lead the overwhelming masses of people, the workers, to develop organisations for self-defense, including labour unions and political parties. Further recessions and contradictions would then spark the working class to overthrow capitalism in a revolution, restructure the economic, political, and social institutions on rational socialist models, and begin the transition towards an eventual communist society. In Marxian terms, the dialectically changing economic base of society would determine the cultural and political superstructure. Although Marx and Engels had famously predicted this eschatological scenario in 1848, many decades later the workers of the industrialised core still had not carried out the mission.

Gramsci argued that the failure of the workers to make an anti-capitalist revolution was due to the successful capture of the workers' ideology, self-understanding, and organisations by the hegemonic (ruling) culture. In other words, the perspective of the ruling class had been absorbed by the masses of workers. In "advanced" industrial societies hegemonic cultural innovations such as compulsory schooling, mass media, and popular culture had indoctrinated workers to a false consciousness. Instead of working towards a revolution that would truly serve their collective needs, workers in "advanced" societies were listening to the rhetoric of nationalist leaders, seeking consumer opportunities and middle-class status, embracing an individualist ethos of success through competition, and/or accepting the guidance of bourgeois religious leaders. Gramsci therefore argued for a strategic distinction between a "war of position" and a "war of movement". The war of position is a culture war in which anti-capitalist elements seek to gain a dominant voice in mass media, mass organisations, and educational institutions to heighten class consciousness, teach revolutionary analysis and theory, and inspire revolutionary organisation. Following the success of the war of position, communist leaders would be empowered to begin the war of movement, the actual insurrection against capitalism, with mass support.

Although the analysis of cultural domination was first advanced in terms of economic classes, it can be applied more broadly. Gramsci's analysis suggested that prevailing cultural norms should not be viewed as "natural" or "inevitable". Rather, cultural norms - including institutions, practices, beliefs - should be investigated for their roots in domination and their implications for liberation.

Gramsci did not contend that hegemony was either monolithic or unified. Instead, hegemony was portrayed as a complex layering of social structures. Each of these structures have their own "mission" and internal logic that allows its members to behave in a way that is different from those in different structures. Yet, as with an army, each of these structures assumes the existence of other structures and by virtue of their differing missions, is able to coalesce and produce a larger structure that has a larger overall mission. This larger mission usually is not exactly the same as the mission for each smaller structure, but it assumes and subsumes them. Hegemony works in the same manner. Each person lives their life in a way that is meaningful in their immediate setting, and, to this person the different parts of society may seem to have little in common with him. Yet taken as a whole, each person's life also contributes to the larger hegemony of the society. Diversity, variation, and free will seem to exist since most people see what they believe to be a plethora of different circumstances, but they miss the larger pattern of hegemony created by the coalescing of these circumstances. Through the existence of small and different circumstances, a larger and layered hegemony is maintained yet not fully recognised by many of the people who live within it.

In such a layered hegemony, individual common sense, which is fragmented, is effective in helping people deal with small, everyday activities. But common sense also inhibits their ability to grasp the larger systemic nature of exploitation and hegemony. People focus on immediate concerns and problems rather than focusing upon more fundamental sources of social oppression.

Although leftists may have been the primary users of this conceptual tool, the activities of organised conservative movements also draw upon the concept. This was seen, for instance, in evangelical Christian efforts to capture local school boards in the U.S. during the 1990s, and thus be able to dictate curriculum. Patrick Buchanan, in a widely discussed speech to the 1992 Republican Convention, used the term "culture war" to describe political and social struggle in the United States.

Theory about hegemonic culture has profoundly influenced Eurocommunism, the social sciences, and activist strategies. In social science the application of the concept of hegemony in the examination of major discourses has become an important aspect of sociology, political science, anthropology, and other cultural studies. In education the concept has led to the development of critical pedagogy.

1.7.2. Contemporary Political Analysis

Cultural hegemony continues to be a widely applied model in political analysis. For example, an analysis of US political power from 1932-2006 speaks to the dynamics of both class struggle and cultural hegemony. In this view, the surge in trade union membership in the 1930s helped create a massive political base for the Democratic Party, one which declined but persisted largely until 1980.

Both material forces in play (such as class and capital), but also a cultural politics, in which ruling interests seek to find emotional issues with which shift worker loyalties from social programmes to those which benefit the largest corporations. Many scholars have used these ideas to explain the rise of Margaret Thatcher in the UK and Ronald Reagan in the US. The pattern of playing to issues of race, fear, and individualism in the US is sometimes represented by the notion of the "Southern strategy." More recently, many scholars have argued that the complex events of September 11, 2001 were instantly and deliberately conflated with "The War on Terror," a tool with which George W. Bush exploited nationalism, racism, Christianity, and fear so as to pursue corporate profiteering in the energy sector, pharmaceuticals, armaments, telecommunications, and other key sectors.

1.7.2.1. Cultural assimilation

According to the Encyclopedia of the Social Sciences, Assimilation is the name given to the process or proceses by which people of diverse racial origins and different cultural heritages, occupying a common territory, achieve a cultural solidarity sufficient at least to sustain a national existence.

Therefore it is not the process by which an immigrant group looses its cultural characteristics in order to acquire the ones of the host society. It is the process by which both cultures (immigrant and host) meet and fuse, into an enriched culture.

1.8. Conclusion

The world increasingly is confronted by problems that can not be solved by individual nation-states acting alone. Cross-boundary air and water pollution, over-fishing of the oceans and other degradations of the natural environment, regulation of outer-space, global warming, international terrorist networks, global trade and finance, and so on. Solutions to these problems necessitate new forms of cooperation and the creation of new global institutions.

References

Agnew, John, David N. Livingstone, and Alisdair Rogers, eds., *Human Geography: An Essential Anthology*, Oxford and Cambridge, Mass.: Blackwell, 1996.

Clark, Michael J., Kenneth J. Gregory, and Angela M. Gurnell, eds., *Horizons in Physical Geography*, Basingstoke and London: Macmillan Education, 1987.

Cosgrove, Denis, *Apollo's Eye: A Cartographic Genealogy of the Earth in the Western Imagination*, Baltimore and London: John Hopkins University Press, 2001.

Diamond, Jared, *Guns, Germs, and Steel: The Fates of Human Societies*, New York: Norton, 1999.

Entrikin, J. Nicholas, and Stanley D. Brunn, eds. Reflections on Richard Hartshorne's "The Nature of Geography", Washington, D.C.: Association of American Geographers, 1989.

Haggett, Peter, *Geography: A Modern Synthesis*, 2nd ed., New York: Harper and Row, 1975.

Hartshorne, Richard, *Perspective on the Nature of Geography*, Chicago: Published by Rand McNally and Company as Monograph No. 1, 1959.

_______________, "The Nature of Geography: A Critical Survey of Current Thought in the Light of the Past", Lancaster, Pa.: The Association, 1939.

Harvey, David, *Spaces of the Capital: Towards a Critical Geography*, Edinburgh: Edinburgh University Press, 2001.

Livingston, David N., and Charles W. J. Withers, eds., *Geography and Enlightenment*, Chicago: University of Chicago Press, 1999.

Quaino, Massimo, *Geography and Marxism*, Translated by Alan Braley, Totowa, N.J.: Barnes and Noble, 1982.

Romm, James S., *The Edges of the Earth in Ancient Thought: Geography, Exploration, and Fiction*, Princeton, N.J.: Princeton University Press, 1992.

Thrower, Norman J. W., *Maps and Civilization: Cartography in Culture and Society*, 2nd ed. Chicago and London: University of Chicago Press, 1999.

2

Development Geography

2.1. Introduction

Development geography is the study of the Earth's geography and its relationship with economic development. It is very closely related to economic geography and development economics. Development economics is a branch of economics which largely deals with the economic aspects of the development process in developing countries with a focus on methods of promoting economic growth while also dealing "with the economic, social, political and institutional mechanisms, both public and private, necessary to bring about rapid and large-scale improvements in levels of living for the peoples" living in developing countries. Moreover, development economics is a study which attempts to coordinate the earnings and aspirations of most people. Thus, development economics involves the creation of theories which aid in the determination of types of policies and practices, which can be implemented at either the domestic or international level, that will improve the standard of living for the general population of developing countries. This may involve using mathematical methods from dynamical systems like differential equations and inter-temporal optimisation, or it may involve a mixture of quantitative and qualitative methods. Unlike in many other fields of economics, approaches in development economics may incorporate social and political factors to devise particular plans.

2.2. Theories of Development Economics

2.2.1. Linear-stages-of-growth Model

The earliest theory of development economics, the linear-stages-of-growth model was first formulated in the 1950s by W. W.

Rostow in The Stages of Growth. This theory focuses on the accelerated accumulation of capital, through the utilisation of both domestic and international savings as a means of spurring investment, as the primary means of promoting economic growth and, thus, development. The linear-stages-of-growth model posits that there are a series of five consecutive stages of development which all countries must go through during the process of development. These stages are "the traditional society, the pre-conditions for take-off, the take-off, the drive to maturity, and the age of high mass-consumption" This theory gave further rise to the Harrod-Domar Model which serves to explain through mathematics the basic assumption that improved capital investment leads to greater economic growth.

This theory has been criticised for not recognising that, while necessary, capital accumulation is not a sufficient condition for development. That is to say that this early and simplistic theory failed to account for political, social and institutional obstacles to development. Furthermore, this theory was developed in the early years of the Cold War and was largely derived from the successes of the Marshall Plan. This has led to the major criticism that the theory assumes that the conditions found in developing countries are the same as those found in post-WWII Europe.

2.2.2. Structural-change Theory

Structural-change theory deals with policies focused on changing the economic structures of developing countries from being primarily comprised of subsistence agricultural practices to being a "more modern, more urbanised, and more industrially diverse manufacturing and service economy." There are two major forms of structural-change theory; W. Lewis' two-sector surplus model, which views agrarian societies as consisting of large amounts of surplus labour which can be utilised to spur the development of an urbanised industrial sector, and Hollis Chenery's patterns of development approach, which is the empirical analysis of the "sequential process through which the economic, industrial and institutional structure of an underdeveloped economy is transformed over time to permit new industries to replace traditional agriculture as the engine of economic growth."

Structural-change approaches to development economics have faced criticism for their emphasis on urban development at the expense of rural development which can lead to a substantial rise in inequality between internal regions of a country. The two-sector surplus model, which was developed in the 1950s, has been further criticised for its underlying assumption that predominantly agrarian societies suffer from a surplus of labour. Actual empirical studies have shown that such labour surpluses are only seasonal and drawing such labour to urban areas can result in a collapse of the agricultural sector. The patterns of development approach has been criticised for lacking a theoretical framework.

2.2.3. International Dependence Theory

International dependence theories gained prominence in the 1970s as a reaction to the failure of earlier theories to lead to widespread successes in international development. Unlike earlier theories, international dependence theories have their origins in developing countries and view obstacles to development as being primarily external in nature, rather than internal. These theories view developing countries as being economically and politically dependent on more powerful, developed countries which have an interest in maintaining their dominant position. There are three different, major formulations of international dependence theory; neocolonial dependence theory, the false-paradigm model and the dualistic-dependence model. The first formulation of international dependence theory, neocolonial dependence theory has its origins in Marxism and views the failure of many developing nations to undergo successful development as being the result of the historical development of the international capitalist system.

2.2.4. Neoclassical Theory

First gaining prominency with the rise of several conservative governments in the West during the 1980s, neoclassical theories represents a radical shift away from International Dependence Theories. Neoclassical theories argue that governments should not intervene in the economy; in other words, these theories are claiming that an unobstructed free market is the best means of inducing rapid and successful development. Competitive free markets unrestrained by excessive government regulation are seen as being able to naturally ensure that the allocation of resources occurs with the greatest efficiency possible and the economic growth is raised and stabilised.

It is important to note that there are several different approaches within the realm of neoclassical theory, each with subtle, but important, differences in their views regarding the extent to which the market should be left unregulated. These different takes on neoclassical theory are the free market approach, public-choice theory, and the market-friendly approach. Of the three, both the free-market approach and public-choice theory contend that the market should be totally free, meaning that any intervention by the government is necessarily bad. Public-choice theory is arguably the more radical of the two with its view, closely associated with libertarianism, that governments themselves are rarely good and therefore should be as minimal as possible.

The market-friendly approach, unlike the other two, is a more recent development and is often associated with the World Bank. This approach still advocates free markets but recognises that there are many imperfections in the markets of many developing nations and thus argues that some government intervention is an effective means of fixing such imperfections. This branch of human geography is intertwined with resource distribution and consumption, demographics, soil quality, topography, climate and natural disasters.

2.3. Topography

Topography is the study of Earth's surface features or those of planets, moons, and asteroids. In a broader sense, topography is concerned with local detail in general, including not only relief but also vegetative and human-made features, and even local history and culture. This meaning is less common in America, where topographic maps with elevation contours have made "topography" synonymous with relief. The older sense of Topography as the study of place still has currency in Europe.

Topography specifically involves the recording of relief or terrain, the three-dimensional quality of the surface, and the identification of specific landforms. This is also known as geomorphometry. In modern usage, this involves generation of elevation data in electronic form. It is often considered to include the graphic representation of the landform on a map by a variety of techniques, including contour lines, Hypsometric tints, and relief shading.

The term "topography" originated in Ancient Greece and continued in Ancient Rome, as the detailed description of a place. The word comes from the Greek words topos, place and graphia, writing. In classical literature this refers to writing about a place or places, what is now largely called 'local history'. In Britain and in Europe in general, the word topography is still sometimes used in its original sense.

Detailed military surveys in Britain (beginning in the late eighteenth century) were called Ordnance Surveys, and this term was used into the 20th century as generic for topographic surveys and maps. The earliest scientific surveys in France were called the Cassini maps after the family who produced them over four generations. The term "topographic surveys" appears to be American in origin. The earliest detailed surveys in the United States were made by the "Topographical Bureau of the Army," formed during the War of 1812. After the work of national mapping was assumed by the U.S. Geological Survey in 1878, the term topographical remained as a general term for detailed surveys and mapping programs, and has been adopted by most other nations as standard.

In the 20th century, the term topography started to be used to describe surface description in other fields where mapping in a broader sense is used, particularly in medical fields such as neurology.

2.3.1. Objectives

The objective of topography is to determine the position of any feature or more generally any point in terms of both a horizontal Coordinate system such as latitude and longitude, and altitude. Identifying features and recognising typical landform patterns are also part of the field.

A topographic study may be made for a variety of reasons: military planning and geological exploration have been primary motivators to start survey programmes, but detailed information about terrain and surface features is essential for the planning and construction of any major civil engineering, public works, or reclamation projects.

2.3.2. Techniques of Topography

There are a variety of approaches to studying topography. Which method(s) to use depend on the scale and size of the area under study, its accessibility, and the quality of existing surveys.

2.3.2.1. Direct survey

Surveying helps determine accurately the terrestrial or three-dimensional space position of points and the distances and angles between them using levelling instruments such as theodolites, dumpy levels and clinometers.

Even though remote sensing has greatly speeded up the process of gathering information, and has allowed greater accuracy control over long distances, the direct survey still provides the basic control points and framework for all topographic work, whether manual or GIS-based.

In areas where there has been an extensive direct survey and mapping programme (most of Europe and the Continental US, for example), the compiled data forms the basis of basic digital elevation datasets such as USGS DEM data. This data must often be "cleaned" to eliminate discrepancies between surveys, but it still forms a valuable set of information for large-scale analysis.

The original American topographic surveys involved not only recording of relief, but identification of landmark features and vegetative land cover.

2.3.2.2. Remote sensing

Remote sensing is a general term for geodata collection at a distance from the subject area.

2.3.2.3. Aerial and satellite imagery

Besides their role in photogrammetry, aerial and satellite imagery can be used to identify and delineate terrain features and more general land-cover features. Certainly they have become more and more a part of geovisualisation, whether maps or GIS systems. False-colour and non-visible spectra imaging can also help determine the lie of the land by delineating vegetation and other land-use information more clearly. Images can be in visible colours and in other spectra.

2.3.3. Photogrammetry

Photogrammetry is a measurement technique for which the co-ordinates of the points in 3D of an object are determined by the measurements made in two photographic images (or more) taken starting from different positions, usually from different passes of an aerial photography flight. In this technique, the common points are identified on each image. A line of sight can be built from the camera location to the point on the object. It is the intersection of its rays (triangulation) which determines the relative three-dimensional position of the point. Known control points can be used to give these relative positions absolute values. More sophisticated algorithms can exploit other information on the scene known a priori (for example, symmetries in certain cases allowing the rebuilding of three-dimensional co-ordinates starting from one only position of the camera).

2.3.3.1. Radar and sonar

Satellite radar mapping is one of the major techniques of generating Digital Elevation Models. Similar techniques are applied in bathymetric surveys using sonar to determine the terrain of the ocean floor.

2.3.3.2. Forms of topographic data

Terrain is commonly modelled either using vector (Triangulated Irregular Network or TIN) or gridded mathematical models. In the most applications in environmental sciences, land surface is represented and modelled using gridded models. In civil engineering and entertainment businesses, the most representations of land surface employ some variant of TIN models. In geostatistics, land surface is commonly modelled as a combination of the two signals - the smooth (spatially correlated) and the rough (noise) signal.

In practice, surveyors first sample heights in an area, then use these to produce a Digital Surface Model (also known as a digital elevation model). The DLSM can then be used to visualise terrain, drape remote sensing images, quantify ecological properties of a surface or extract land surface objects. Note that the contour data or any other sampled elevation datasets are not a DLSM. A DLSM implies that elevation is available continuously at each location in the study area, i.e. that the map represents a complete surface. Digital Land Surface Models should not be confused with Digital Surface Models, which can be surfaces of the canopy, buildings and similar objects. For example, in the case of surface models produces using the LIDAR technology, one can have several surfaces - starting from the top of the canopy to the actual solid earth. The difference between the two surface models can then be used to derive volumetric measures (height of trees etc).

2.3.3.3. Raw survey data

Topographic survey information is historically based upon the notes of surveyors. They may derive naming and cultural information from other local sources for example, boundary delineation may be derived from local cadastral mapping. While of historical interest, these field notes inherently include errors and contradictions that later stages in map production resolve.

2.3.3.4. Remote sensing data

As with field notes, remote sensing data (aerial and satellite photography), is raw and uninterpreted. It may contain holes (due to cloud cover for example) or inconsistencies (due to the timing of specific image captures). Most modern topographic mapping includes a large component of remotely sensed data in its compilation process.

2.3.4. Topographic Mapping

In its contemporary definition, topographic mapping shows relief. In the United States, USGS topographic maps show relief using contour lines. The USGS calls maps based on topographic surveys, but without contours, "planimetric maps."

These maps show not only the contours, but also any significant streams or other bodies of water, forest cover, built-up areas or individual buildings (depending on scale), and other features and points of interest.

While not officially "topographic" maps, the national surveys of other nations share many of the same features, and so they are often generally called "topographic maps."

Existing topographic survey maps, because of their comprehensive and encyclopedic coverage, form the basis for much derived topographic work. Digital Elevation Models, for example, have often been created not from new remote sensing data but from existing paper topographic maps. Many government and private publishers use the artwork (especially the countour lines) from existing topographic map sheets as the basis for their own specialised or updated topographic maps.

Topographic mapping should not be confused with Geologic mapping. The latter is concerned with underlying structures and processes to the surface, rather than with identifiable surface features.

2.3.4.1. Digital elevation modelling

The digital elevation model (DEM) is a raster-based digital dataset of the topography (altimetry and/or bathymetry) of all or part of the Earth (or a telluric planet). The pixels of the dataset are each assigned an elevation value, and a header portion of the dataset defines the are of coverage, the units each pixel covers, and the units of elevation (and the zero-point). DEMs may be derived from exisitng paper maps and survey data, or they may be generated from new satellite or other remotely-sensed radar or sonar data.

2.3.4.2. Topological modelling

A geographic information system (GIS) can recognise and analyse the spatial relationships that exist within digitally stored spatial data. These topological relationships allow complex spatial modelling and analysis to be performed. Topological relationships between geometric entities traditionally include adjacency (what adjoins what), containment (what encloses what), and proximity (how close something is to something else).

— reconstitute a sight in synthesised images of the ground,
— determine a trajectory of overflight of the ground,
— calculate surfaces or volumes,
— trace topographic profiles,
— handle in a quantitative way the studied ground.

2.4. Climate

Climate is the average and variations of weather over long periods of time. Climate zones can be defined using parameters such as temperature and rainfall. Paleoclimatology focuses on ancient climate information derived from sediment found in lake beds, ice cores, as well as various fauna and flora including tree rings and coral. Climate models can be used to determine the amount of climate change anticipated in the future.

Climate is commonly defined as the weather averaged over a long period of time. The standard averaging period is 30 years but other periods may be used depending on the purpose. Climate also includes statistics other than the average, such as the magnitudes of day-to-day or year-to-year variations. The Intergovernmental Panel on Climate Change (IPCC) glossary definition is: Climate in a narrow sense is usually defined as the "average weather", or more rigorously, as the statistical description in terms of the mean and variability of relevant quantities over a period of time ranging from months to thousands or millions of years. The classical period is 30 years, as defined by the World Meteorological Organisation (WMO). These quantities are most often surface variables such as temperature, precipitation, and wind. Climate in a wider sense is the state, including a statistical description, of the climate system.

The main difference between climate and everyday weather is best summarised by the popular phrase "Climate is what you expect, weather is what you get." Over historic time spans there are a number of static variables that determine climate, including: latitude, altitude, proportion of land to water, and proximity to oceans and mountains. Other climate determinants are more dynamic: The thermohaline circulation of the ocean distributes heat energy between the equatorial and polar regions; other ocean currents do the same between land and water on a more regional scale. Degree of vegetation coverage affects solar heat absorption, water retention, and rainfall on a regional level. Alterations in the quantity of atmospheric greenhouse gases determines the amount of solar energy retained by the planet, leading to global warming or global cooling. The variables which determine climate are numerous and the interactions complex, but there is general agreement that the broad outlines are understood, at least insofar as the determinants of historical climate change are concerned.

2.4.1. Classifications

In the original Greek sense, 'Clime,' was a concept used to divide the world into climatic zones sharing similar climatic attributes such as temperature, length of the solar day (sunlight), and in particular latitudinal distance from the equator. Modern data and analysis show that the latitudinal concepts of antiquity are too simplistic. Instead, the latitudinal trend is altered by such features as hills or mountain ranges, large lakes, and seas or oceans.

Consequently, today's climate regions are classified on the basis of temperature and precipitation alone. Classification schemes usually seek a close correspondence between climate regions and vegetation biomes. The most commonly used classification is the Köppen classification system, which divides Earth's climates into five (sometimes six) primary classes and numerous subclasses. Another classification system is the Thornthwaite climate classification. In broad terms, climate zones range in latitude from tropical (hot, no real seasons based on temperature) to mid-latitude (moderate; conventional winter-spring-summer-autumn seasons) to polar (cold; strong seasonality; long winters). They also divide into continental (high contrast between summer and winter) and maritime (ocean influence moderates temperature extremes, but generally contribute extra moisture to local weather patterns). The mid-latitude 'conventional four seasons' only work well in the mid-latitudes. In other regions, the more useful divide is into "wet" and "dry" seasons based on the monsoon.

Worldwide climate classifications are—Tropical climate, Subtropical climate, Arid climate, Semiarid climate, Mediterranean climate, Temperate climate, Oceanic climate, Continental climate, Alpine climate, Subarctic climate, Polar climate, Climate of Antarctica and Köppen climate classification.

2.4.2. Climate Record

2.4.2.1. *Modern*

Details of the modern climate record are known through the taking of measurements from such weather instruments as thermometers, barometers, and anemometers during the past few centuries. The instruments used to study weather conditions over the modern time scale, their known error, their immediate environment, and their exposure have changed over the years, which must be considered when studying the climate of centuries past.

2.4.2.2. *Paleoclimatology*

Paleoclimatology is the study of climate change taken on a longer scale, spanning a greater section of the Earth's history. It uses records from ice sheets, tree rings, sediment, coral, and rocks to determine the past state of the climate system on Earth, and whether or not long term climate cycles exist.

2.4.3. Climate Change

Climate change refers to the variation in the Earth's global climate or in regional climates over time. It describes changes in the variability or average state of the atmosphere over time scales ranging from decades to millions of years. These changes can be caused by processes internal to the Earth, external forces or, more recently, human activities.

In recent usage, especially in the context of environmental policy, the term "climate change" often refers only to changes in modern climate, including the rise in average surface temperature known as global warming. In some cases, the term is also used with a presumption of human causation, as in the United Nations Framework Convention on Climate Change (UNFCCC). The UNFCCC uses "climate variability" for non-human caused variations.

Earth has undergone periodic climate shifts in the past, including four major ice ages. These consisting of glacial periods where conditions are colder than normal, separated by interglacial periods. The accumulation of snow and ice during a glacial period increases the surface albedo, reflecting more of the Sun's energy into space and maintaining a lower atmospheric temperature. Increases in greenhouse gases, such as by volcanic activity, can increase the global temperature and produce an interglacial. Suggested causes of ice age periods include the positions of the continents, variations in the Earth's orbit, changes in the solar output, and vulcanism.

2.4.3.1. Climate models

Climate models use quantitative methods to simulate the interactions of the atmosphere, oceans, land surface, and ice. They are used for a variety of purposes from study of the dynamics of the weather and climate system to projections of future climate. All climate models balance, or very nearly balance, incoming energy as short wave (including visible) electromagnetic radiation to the earth with outgoing energy as long wave (infrared) electromagnetic radiation from the earth. Any unbalance results in a change in the average temperature of the earth.

The most talked-about models of recent years have been those relating temperature to emissions of carbon dioxide. These models predict an upward trend in the surface temperature record, as well as a more rapid increase in temperature at higher altitudes.

2.4.4. Measuring Development

There are many methods that geographers use to quantify and compare the development of different countries and they have different strengths and weaknesses. Quantitative Indicators are numerical indications of development.

Gross National Product (GNP) (a close value is Gross National Income, equal to GNP + depreciation allowances) is the total value of all final goods and services produced by a country's factors of production and sold on the market in a given time period.

Nominal GNP measures the value of output during a given year using the prices prevailing during that year. Over time, the general level of prices rise due to inflation, leading to an increase in nominal GNP even if the volume of goods and services produced is unchanged. GNP does not include goods produced on a subsistence level, i.e. farmers who eat their own products do not have their crops included in the GNP.

Real GNP measures the value of output in two or more different years by valuing the goods and services adjusted for inflation. For example, if both the "nominal GNP" and price level doubled between 1995 and 2005, the "real GNP" would remain the same. For year over year GNP growth, "real GNP" is usually used because it gives a more accurate view of the economy. It also has nothing to do with the population.

Gross Domestic Product (GDP) is the total value of final goods and services produced within a country's borders in a year. GDP counts income according to where it is earned rather than who owns the factors of production. In the above example, all of the income from the (German-owned) car factory would be counted as Belgian GDP rather than German GDP. To convert from GNP to GDP you must subtract net factor income receipts from foreigners that correspond to goods and services produced abroad using factor inputs supplied by domestic sources.

2.4.4.1. National income and welfare

GNP per person is often used as a measure of people's welfare. Countries with higher GNP often score highly on other measures of welfare, such as life expectancy. However, there are serious limitations to the usefulness of GNP as a measure of welfare:

— Measures of GNP typically exclude unpaid economic activity, most importantly domestic work such as childcare. This can lead to distortions.

— GNP takes no account of the inputs used to produce the output.

— Comparison of GNP from one country to another may be distorted by movements in exchange rates. Measuring national income at purchasing power parity can help to overcome this problem at the risk of overvaluing basic goods and services like subsistence farming.

— GNP does not take into account many factors that may be important to quality of life, such as the quality of the environment and security from crime. This can lead to distortions.

— GNP is the mean wealth rather than median wealth. Countries with a skewed income distribution may have a relatively high per-capita GNP while the majority of its citizens have a relatively low level of income, due to concentration of wealth in the hands of a small fraction of the population.

— GNP per capita measures the value of all the goods and services produced in a country, excluding those produced by foreign companies. This figure is widely used but has many problems. GNP does not measure whether the money produced is actually improving people's lives and this is important because in many MEDCs where there are large increases in wealth over time but only small increases in happiness. In LEDCs it is often too expensive to accurately collect this data and some governments intentionally or unintentionally release inaccurate figures.

The Purchasing power parity (PPP) theory was developed by Gustav Cassel in 1920. It is the method of using the long-run equilibrium exchange rate of two currencies to equalise the currencies' purchasing power. It is based on the law of one price, the idea that, in an efficient market, identical goods must have only one price.

Purchasing power parity is often called absolute purchasing power parity to distinguish it from a related theory relative purchasing power parity, which predicts the relationship between the two countries' relative inflation rates and the change in the exchange rate of their currencies.

A purchasing power parity exchange rate equalises the purchasing power of different currencies in their home countries for a given basket of goods. These special exchange rates are often used to compare the standards of living of two or more countries. The adjustments are meant to give a better picture than comparing gross domestic products (GDP) using market exchange rates. This type of adjustment to an exchange rate is controversial because of the difficulties of finding comparable baskets of goods to compare purchasing power across countries.

Market exchange rates fluctuate widely, but many believe that PPP exchange rates reflect the long run equilibrium value. The distortions caused by using market rates are accentuated because prices of non-traded goods and services are usually lower in poorer economies. The differences between PPP and market exchange rates can be significant.

Estimation of purchasing power parity is complicated by the fact that countries do not simply differ in a uniform price level; rather, the difference in food prices may be greater than the difference in housing prices, while also less than the difference in entertainment prices. People in different countries typically consume different baskets of goods. It is necessary to compare the cost of baskets of goods and services using a price index. This is a difficult task because purchasing patterns and even the goods available to purchase differ across countries. Thus, it is necessary to make adjustments for differences in the quality of goods and services. Additional statistical difficulties arise with multilateral comparisons when more than two countries are to be compared. When PPP comparisons are to be made over some interval of time, proper account needs to be made of inflationary effects.

2.4.4.2. *Relative PPP*

Relative PPP relates the inflation rate (the change of price levels) in each country to the change in the market exchange rate. According to this theory, the change in the exchange rate is determined by price level changes in both countries.

The law of one price states that differing prices of a traded good will tend to equalise in the absence of tariffs, other barriers to trade and prohibitively high shipping rates. The law of one price can also be stated as: "In an efficient market all identical goods must have only one price." The naïve PPP hypothesis is that free trade of goods should revert exchange rates to their PPP values. However, econometric analysis rejects this hypothesis, and gives a better prediction of the PPP/exchange rate relationship (the CPI) based on relative GDPs. Neo-classical economics includes Balassa-Samuelson effect theory, which explains the PPP model adjustment giving the equilibrium CPIs.

2.4.4.3. *Big Mac Index*

An entertaining example of one measure of PPP is the Big Mac Index popularised by The Economist, which looks at the prices of a Big Mac burger in McDonald's restaurants in different countries. The Big Mac Index is presumably useful because it is based on a well-known good whose final price, easily tracked in many countries, includes input costs from a wide range of sectors in the local economy, such as agricultural commodities (beef, bread, lettuce, tomatoes), labour (blue and white collar), advertising, rent and real estate costs, transportation, etc.

2.4.4.4. iPod Index

The Australian securities firm CommSec introduced the iPod Index as a light-hearted method of measuring PPP. Unlike the Big Mac, which is affected by local labour and transport costs, the iPod manufacturing costs are the same and the iPod is a tradable commodity.

2.4.5. Need for PPP Adjustments to GDP

Using market exchange rates to compare countries' standard of living or per capita Gross Domestic Product can give a very misleading picture. The exchange rate only reflects traded goods in contrast to non-traded ones. Also, currencies are traded for purposes other than trade in goods and services, e.g., to buy capital assets whose prices vary more than those of physical goods. Also, different interest rates, speculation, hedging or interventions by central banks can influence the foreign-exchange market. The PPP method is used as an alternative.

PPP exchange rates are especially useful when official exchange rates are artificially manipulated by governments. Countries with strong government control of the economy sometimes enforce official exchange rates that make their own currency artificially strong. By contrast, the currency's black market exchange rate is artificially weak. In such cases a PPP exchange rate is likely the most realistic basis for economic comparison.

2.4.5.1. Difficulties

The main reasons why PPP does not perfectly reflect standards of living are:

- — birth rate, death rate and fertility rate. birth rate, death rate and fertility rate. PPP numbers can vary with the specific basket of goods used, making it a rough estimate.

— Preferences and choices can vary from country to country. Goods then differ in their contribution to welfare.

— International competitiveness is mainly affected by the exchange rate and not by PPP.

— Differences in quality of goods are not sufficiently reflected in PPP.

— The price of a product within one currency-zone may vary drastically.

— Imported goods are purchased at market exchange rates, and thus a country that has to import all of its food would appear better off than it actually is if the PPP is used as the measurement of well-being.

— There is no single global market, so "in an efficient market, identical goods must have only one price" is no better than a platitude. Prices are dependent upon the interplay between supply and demand, and these vary from time to time and place to place.

More processed and expensive products are likely to be tradable, falling into the second category, and drifting from the PPP exchange rate to the currency exchange rate. Even if the PPP "value" of the Chinese currency is five times stronger than the currency exchange rate, it won't buy five times as much of internationally traded goods like steel, cars and microchips, but non-traded goods like housing, services, and domestically produced rice. The relative price differential between tradables and non-tradables from high-income to low-income countries is a consequence of the Balassa-Samuelson effect, and gives a big cost advantage to labour intensive production of tradable goods in low income countries (like China), as against high income countries (like Switzerland). The corporate cost advantage is nothing more sophisticated than access to cheaper workers, but because the pay of those workers goes further in low-income countries than high, the relative pay differentials (inter-country) can be sustained for longer than would be the case otherwise. An equivalent cost benefit comes from non-traded goods that can be sourced locally. These act as a relatively cheaper factor of production than is available to factories in richer countries. PPP calculations tend to overemphasise the primary sectoral contribution and underemphasise the industrial and service sectoral contributions to the economy of a nation.

2.4.6. Difficulties with PPP Comparisons in Welfare Economics

While using PPP exchange rates for income comparison is an improvement over using market exchange rates, it is still imperfect, and comparisons using the PPP method can still be misleading. Comparing standards of living using the PPP method implicitly assumes that the real value placed on goods is the same in different countries. In reality, what is considered a luxury in one culture could be considered a necessity in another. The PPP method does not account for this.

A PPP exchange rate varies depending on the choice of goods used for the index (CPI). Hence, it is possible to deliberately or accidentally bias a PPP exchange rate by the choice of a bundle. Indeed, it may be hard to construct equivalent representative bundles for the consumption habits of very different societies. PPP could also have difficulty accounting for differences in quality between goods in one country and equivalent goods in another.

Differing levels of government involvement in social spheres further complicate development of good CPI baskets (and, consequently, PPP measurements).

Even if a good PPP is used, GDP per capita is still a measure of the economic output of the whole economy, not a direct measure of the mean or median person's quality of life. Other factors such as the standards of homes and schools, access to public services, the extent of pollution, and strength of consumer protection laws are hard to quantify and generally not fully reflected in the GDP. Even a PPP-adjusted measure of GDP per capita must be used with caution, for all the usual reasons that the GDP figure itself is limited. While per-capita income does not take into account inequalities in wealth distribution, neither does the PPP-scaled income.

2.4.6.1. Clarification to PPP Numbers of the IMF

The GDP number for all reporting areas are one number in the reporting areas local currency. Therefore, in the local currency the PPP and market (or government) exchange rate is always 1.0 to its own currency, so the PPP and market exchange rate GDP number is always per definition the same for any duration of time, anytime, in that area's currency. The only time the PPP exchange rate and the market exchange rate can differ is when the GDP number is converted into another currency.

2.4.6.2. Total fertility rate

The total fertility rate (TFR) of a population is the average number of children that would be born to a woman over her lifetime if she were to experience the exact current age-specific fertility rates (ASFRs) through her lifetime. It is obtained by summing the age-specific rates for a given time-point.

The TFR is a synthetic rate, not something that is actually counted. It is not based on the fertility of any real group of women, since this would involve waiting until they had completed childbearing. Nor is it based on counting up the total number of children actually born over their lifetime, but instead is based on the age-specific fertility rates of women in their "child-bearing years," which in conventional international statistical usage is ages 15-44 or 15-49.

The TFR is therefore a measure of the fertility of an imaginary woman who passes through her reproductive life subject to all the age-specific fertility rates for ages 15-49 that were recorded for a given population in a given year. The TFR represents the average number of children a woman would have were she to fast-forward through all her childbearing years in a single year, assuming the all the age-specific fertility rates for that year. In other words, this rate is the number of children a woman would have if she was subject to prevailing fertility rates at all ages from a single given year, and survives throughout all her childbearing years.

An alternative fertility measure is the net reproduction rate (NRR), which measures the number of daughters a woman would have in her lifetime if she were subject to prevailing age-specific fertility and mortality rates in the given year. When the NRR is exactly one then each generation of women is exactly reproducing itself. The NRR is less widely used than the TFR, and the United Nations stopped reporting NRR data for member nations after 1998. But the NRR is particularly relevant where the number of male babies born is very high. The gross reproduction rate (GRR), is the same as the NRR, except that - like the TFR - it ignores life expectancy.

The TFR (or TPFR) is a better index of fertility than the Crude birth rate (annual number of births per thousand population) because it is independent of the age structure of the population, but it is a poorer estimate of actual completed family size than the total cohort fertility rate, which is obtained by summing the age-specific fertility rates that actually applied to each cohort as they aged through time. In particular, the TFR does not necessarily predict how many children young women now will eventually have, as their fertility rates in years to come may change from those of older women now. However, the TFR is a reasonable summary of current fertility levels.

2.4.6.3. Replacement rates

Replacement fertility is the total fertility rate at which women would have only enough children to replace themselves and their partner. By definition, replacement is only considered to have occurred when the offspring reach 15 years of age. If there were no mortality in the female population until the end of the childbearing years then the replacement rate would be exactly 2, but in practice it is affected by mortality, especially childhood mortality.

2.5. Conclusion

As the world is divided into the More Economically Developed Countries and Less Economically Developed Countries wealth (both money and materials resources) is unequally distributed among the world's population with large consequences for people's lifestyles and the environment. In development geography, geographers study spatial patterns in development and try to find by what characteristics they can measure economic development. They seek to understand both the geographical causes and consequences of varying development.

Developed countries usually have a much lower fertility rate due to greater wealth and their individualistic culture. Mortality rates are low, birth control is easily accessible, and human beings are often deemed (by other human beings) as nothing but an economic drain, specially when they cannot produce income: because of education costs, clothing and feeding. Longer periods of time spent getting higher education often mean young people have children later in life. The result is the demographic-economic paradox.

In developing countries on the other hand, families desire children for their labour and as caregivers for their parents in old age. Fertility rates are also higher due to the lack of access to contraceptives, generally lower levels of female education, and lower rates of female employment in industry.

References

Meyer-Arendt, K.J., "Historical Coastal Environmental Changes: Human Response to Shoreline Erosion", in *The American Environment: Interpretations of Past Geographies* (L. Dilsaver & C. Colten, eds.), Savage, MD: Rowman & Littlefield, 1992.

Nordstrom, K.F. and Jackson, N. L., "Temporal and spatial scales of landscape change following storms on human-altered coasts", *Journal of Coastal Conservation*, 1995.

Phillips, J. D., "Human agency, Holocene sea level, and floodplain accretion in coastal plain rivers", *Journal of Coastal Research*, 1997.

Vallega, A., "Ocean geography vis-à-vis global change and sustainable development", *The Professional Geographer*, 1999.

Walker, H. J., "The coastal zone", In *The Earth as Transformed by Human Action*, ed. B. L. Turner, Cambridge: Cambridge University Press, 1990.

Walker, H. J., "Nature, humans, and the coastal zone", *The International Journal of Social Education*, 1990.

3

Behavioural Geography

Behavioural geography is an approach to Human Geography that examines human behaviour using a desegregate approach. Behavioural Geographers focus on the cognitive processes underlying spatial reasoning, decision making, and behaviour. Because of the name it is often incorrectly assumed to have its roots in behaviourism. Due to the emphasis on cognition, this is clearly not the case.

The cognitive processes include environmental perception and cognition, wayfinding, the construction of cognitive maps, place attachment, the development of attitudes about space and place, decisions and behaviour based on imperfect knowledge of one's environs, and numerous other topics. The approach adopted in behavioural geography is closely related to that of psychology, but draws on research findings from a multitude of other disciplines including economics, sociology, anthropology, transportation planning, and many others.

3.1. Critical Geography

The development of critical geography can be seen as one of the four major turning points in the history of geography (the other three being environmental determinism, regional geography and quantitative revolution). Though post-positivist approaches remain important in geography the critical geography arose as a critique of positivism introduced by quantitative revolution.

Two main schools of thought emerged from human geography and one existing school (behavioural geography) which made a brief comeback. Behavioural geography sought to counter the perceived tendency of quantitative geography to deal with humanity as a statistical phenomenon. It flourished briefly during the 1970s and sought to provide a greater understanding of how people perceived places and made locational decisions and sought to challenge mathematical models of society, in particular the use of econometric techniques. But the lack of a sound theoretical base left behavioural geography open to critique as merely descriptive and amounting to little more than a listing of spatial preferences.

Radical geography emerged during the 1970s and 1980s as the inadequacies of behaviouralist methods became clear. It sought to counter the positivist quantitative methods with normative techniques drawn from Marxist theory: quantitative methods, it argued, were not useful unless alternatives or solutions were given to problems.

The final and, arguably, most successful of the three schools was humanistic geography, initially formed part of behavioural geography but fundamentally disagreed with the use of quantitative methods in assessing human behaviour and thoughts in favour of qualitative analysis. Humanistic geography used many of the techniques that the humanities use such as source analysis and the use of text and literature to try to 'get into the mind' of the subject(s). Furthermore, Cultural geography revived due to humanistic geography new areas of study such as Feminist geography, postmodernist and poststructuralist geography began to emerge.

3.2. Culture theory

Culture theory is the branch of anthropology and other related social science disciplines (e.g., sociology) that seeks to define the heuristic concept of culture in operational and/or scientific terms. In the 19th century, "culture" was used by some to refer to a wide array of human activities, and by others as a synonym for "civilisation". In the 20th century, anthropologists began theorising about culture as an object of scientific analysis. Some used it to distinguish human adaptive strategies from the largely instinctive adaptive strategies of animals, including the adaptive strategies of other primates and non-human hominids, whereas others used it to refer to symbolic representations and expressions of human experience, with no direct adaptive value. Both groups understood culture as being definitive of human nature.

According to many theories that have gained wide acceptance among anthropologists, culture exhibits the way that humans interpret their biology and their environment. According to this point of view, culture becomes such an integral part of human existence that it *is* the human environment, and most cultural change can be attributed to human adaptation to historical events. Moreover, given that culture is seen as the primary adaptive mechanism of humans and takes place much faster than human biological evolution, most cultural change can be viewed as culture adapting to itself.

Although most anthropologists try to define culture in such a way that it separates human beings from other animals, many human traits are similar to those of other animals, particularly the traits of other primates. For example, chimpanzees have big brains, but human brains are bigger. Similarly, bonobos exhibit complex sexual behaviour, but human beings exhibit much more complex sexual behaviours. As such, anthropologists often debate whether human behaviour is different from animal behaviour in degree rather than in kind; they must also find ways to distinguish cultural behaviour from sociological behaviour and psychological behaviour.

3.3. Feminist Geography

Feminist geography is an approach to study in human geography which applies the theories, methods and critiques of feminism to the study of the human environment, society and geographical space. Feminist geography is often considered part of a broader postmodern approach to the subject which is not primarily concerned with the development of conceptual theory in itself but rather focuses on the real experiences of individuals and groups in their own localities, upon the geographies that they live in within their own communities.

There are a number of strands to feminist geography, which are not completely distinct, and include:

— Geographic differences in gender relations and gender equality

— The geography of women - spatial constraints, welfare geography

— The construction of gender identity through the use and nature of spaces and places
— Geographies of sexuality.

3.4. Marxist Geography

Marxist geography is a critical geography which utilises the theories and philosophy of Marxism to examine the spatial relations of human geography. Marxist geography, like other critical geographies, grew in response to the "quantitative revolution" and its positivist philosophical underpinnings.

3.4.1. Philosophy and Methodology

Marxist geography is radical in nature and its primary criticism of the positivist spatial science centered upon its methodologies, which failed to account or demonstrate the underlying mechanisms of capitalism and exploitation that underly human spatial arrangements. As such, early Marxist geographers were explicitly political in advocating for social change and activism; they sought, through application of geographical analysis of social problems, to alleviate poverty and exploitation in capitalist societies. Marxist geography makes exegetical claims regarding how the deep-seated structures of capitalism act as a determinants and a constraints to human agency. Most of these ideas were developed in the early 1970s by dissatisfied quantitative geographers; David Harvey is generally regarded as the primary trail-blazer of the Marxist movement in human geography.

In order to accomplish such philosophical aims, these geographers rely heavily upon Marxist social and economic theory; drawing on Marxian economics and the concept of historical materialism to tease out the manner in which the means of production control human spatial distribution in capitalist structures. Marx is also invoked to examine how spatial relationships are affected by class. The emphasis is upon structure and structural mechanisms; emphasis on this aspect of society has yielded results but also criticism.

Marxist geography's emphasis on constraints of structure upon human agency has been criticised extensively as deterministic; not allowing for the human agency and autonomy, whose action appears determined by capitalism's structural mechanisms in Marxist analysis. By contrast, Humanistic geography is a differing critical geography, which concentrates upon human will and autonomy in explaining geography's patterns. Unsurprisingly, much of the criticism directed at Marxists has emerged from the humanistic fold (though humanistic geography is itself seen as lacking for failing to account for behavioural constraints imposed by social structures).

Marxist geography is also subject to critiques of historical materialism and its applicability to modern day post-industrial and capitalist societies. The importance Marxists place on the notion of class is also subject to critique. Marxist geographers have responded in kind to these polemics.

3.5. Modernism

Modernism describes a series of reforming cultural movements in art and architecture, music, literature and the applied arts which emerged in the three decades before 1914.

It is a trend of thought that affirms the power of human beings to create, improve, and reshape their environment, with the aid of scientific knowledge, technology and practical experimentation, and is thus in its essence both progressive and optimistic. The term covers many political, cultural and artistic movements rooted in the changes in Western society at the end of the nineteenth and beginning of the twentieth century. But Modernism encouraged the re-examination of every aspect of existence, from commerce to philosophy, with the goal of finding that which was "holding back" progress, and replacing it with new, progressive and therefore better, ways of reaching the same end.

In essence, the modernist movement argued that the new realities of the industrial and mechanised age were permanent and imminent, and that people should adapt their world view to accept that the new equaled the good, the true and the beautiful. Modern (quantum and relativistic) physics, modern (analytical and continental) philosophy and modern number theory in mathematics are, however, also said to date from this period. Embracing change and the present, modernism encompasses the works of thinkers who rebelled against nineteenth century academic and historicist traditions, believing the "traditional" forms of art, architecture, literature, religious faith, social organisation and daily life were becoming outdated; they directly confronted the new economic, social and political aspects of an emerging fully industrialised world. Some divide the 20th Century into movements designated Modernism and Postmodernism, whereas others see them as two aspects of the same movement.

The first half of the nineteenth century for Europe was marked by a number of wars and revolutions, which reveal the rise of the ideas and doctrines now identified as Romanticism: emphasis on individual subjective experience, the sublime, the supremacy of "Nature" as a subject for art, revolutionary or radical extensions of expression, and individual liberty. By mid-century, however, a synthesis of these ideas with stable governing forms had emerged, partly in reaction to the failed Romantic and democratic Revolutions of 1848. It was exemplified by Otto von Bismarck's *Realpolitik* and by "practical" philosophical ideas such as positivism. Called by various names — in Great Britain it is designated the "Victorian era" — this stabilising synthesis was rooted in the idea that reality dominates over impressions that are subjective.

Central to this synthesis were common assumptions and institutional frames of reference, including the religious norms found in Christianity, scientific norms found in classical physics, especially electromagnetism, and doctrines that asserted that the depiction of external reality from an objective standpoint was not only possible but desirable. Cultural critics and historians label this set of doctrines Realism, though this term is not universal. In philosophy, the rationalist, materialist and positivist movements established a primacy of reason and system.

Against the current ran a series of ideas, some of them direct continuations of Romantic schools of thought. Notable were the agrarian and revivalist movements in plastic arts and poetry. Rationalism also drew responses from the anti-rationalists in philosophy. In particular, Hegel's dialectic view of civilisation and history drew responses from Friedrich Nietzsche and Søren Kierkegaard, who were major influences on Existentialism. All of these separate reactions together began to be seen as offering a challenge to any comfortable ideas of certainty derived by civilisation, history, or pure reason.

From the 1870s onward, the ideas that history and civilisation were inherently progressive and that progress was always good came under increasing attack. Writers Wagner and Ibsen had been reviled for their own critiques of contemporary civilisation and for their warnings that accelerating "progress" would lead to the creation of individuals detached from social norms and isolated from their fellow men. Arguments arose that not merely were the values of the artist and those of society different, but that Society was antithetical to Progress, and could not move forward in its present form. Philosophers called into question the previous optimism. The work of Schopenhauer was labelled "pessimistic" for its idea of the "negation of the will", an idea that would be both rejected and incorporated by later thinkers such as Nietzsche.

Two of the most disruptive thinkers of the period were, in biology, Charles Darwin and, in political science, Karl Marx. Darwin's theory of evolution by natural selection undermined religious certainty of the general public, and the sense of human uniqueness of the intelligentsia. The notion that human beings were driven by the same impulses as "lower animals" proved to be difficult to reconcile with the idea of an ennobling spirituality. Karl Marx seemed to present a political version of the same proposition: that problems with the economic order were not transient, the result of specific wrong doers or temporary conditions, but were fundamentally contradictions within the "capitalist" system. Both thinkers would spawn defenders and schools of thought that would become decisive in establishing modernism.

Separately, in the arts and letters, two ideas originating in France would have particular impact. The first was Impressionism, a school of painting that initially focused on work done, not in studios, but outdoors (*en plein air*). Impressionist paintings demonstrated that human beings do not see objects, but instead see light itself. The school gathered adherents despite internal divisions among its leading practitioners, and became increasingly influential.

At the same time social, political, and economic forces were at work that would become the basis to argue for a radically different kind of art and thinking. Chief among these was steam-powered industrialisation, which produced buildings that combined art and engineering in new industrial materials such as cast iron to produce railroad bridges and glass-and-iron train sheds— or the Eiffel Tower, which broke all previous limitations on how tall man-made objects could be—and at the same time offered a radically different environment in urban life.

The miseries of industrial urbanism, and the possibilities created by scientific examination of subjects brought changes that would shake a European civilisation which had, until then, regarded itself as having a continuous and progressive line of development from the Renaissance. With the telegraph's harnessing of a new power, offering instant communication at a distance, the experience of time itself was altered.

The breadth of the changes can be sensed in how many modern disciplines are described, in their pre-twentieth century form, as being "classical", including physics, economics, and arts such as ballet or architecture.

3.6. Postmodernism

Postmodernism is a term applied to a wide-ranging set of developments in critical theory, philosophy, architecture, art, literature, and culture, which are generally characterised as either emerging from, in reaction to, or superseding, modernism.

Postmodernism was originally a reaction to modernism (not "post" in the purely temporal sense of "after"). Largely influenced by the disillusionment induced by the Second World War, postmodernism tends to refer to a cultural, intellectual, or artistic state lacking a clear central hierarchy or organising principle and embodying extreme complexity, contradiction, ambiguity, diversity, and interconnectedness or interreferentiality.

Postmodernity is a derivative referring to non-art aspects of history that were influenced by the new movement, namely the evolutions in society, economy and culture since the 1960s. When the idea of a reaction to - or even a rejection of - the movement of modernism (a late 19th, early 20th centuries art movement) was borrowed by other fields, it became synonymous in some contexts with postmodernity.

The term was coined in 1949 to describe a dissatisfaction with modern architecture, leading to the postmodern architecture movement. Later, the term was applied to several movements, including in art, music, and literature, that reacted against modern movements, and are typically marked by revival of traditional elements and techniques. Postmodernism in architecture is marked by the re-emergence of surface ornament, reference to surrounding buildings in urban architecture, historical reference in decorative forms, and non-orthogonal angles. It may be a response to the modernist architectural movement known as the International Style.

If used in other contexts, it is a concept without a universally accepted, short and simple definition; in a variety of contexts it is used to describe social conditions, movements in the arts, and scholarship (incl. criticism) in *reaction to modernism.*

Postmodernism is a movement of ideas arising from, but also critical of elements of modernism. Because of the wide range of uses of the term, different elements of modernity are viewed as being coterminous; and different elements of modernity are held to be critiqued. Each of the different usages of 'postmodernism' is also inevitably related to some argument about the nature of knowledge, known in philosophy as epistemology. Individuals who invoke the expression nowadays are implicitly arguing either that there is something fundamentally different about the transmission of meaning in postmodern works of art; or else that there inheres in modernism certain fundamental flaws in its epistemology.

The argument against the need for the concept is that the "modern" era has not yet arrived at its term; and that the most important social and political project of our age remains modernism's project of replacing counter-enlightenment and emotionalist tendencies, as well as combating widesperead cultural ignorance, pervasive superstition, and mindless resistance to technological and social innovations. From this perspective, the realities of the modern era, and its philosophical underpinnings, are being challenged by a backlash from precisely that reactionary quarter against which modernism in fact began its initial late 19th-century crusade.

Postmodernist scholars argue that a global, decentralised society such as ours inevitably creates responses/perceptions that are described as postmodern, such as the rejection of what are seen as the false, imposed unities of meta-narrative and hegemony; the breaking of traditional frames of genre, structure and stylistic unity; and the overthrowing of categories that are the result of logocentrism and other forms of artificially imposed order. Scholars who accept the division of postmodernity as a distinct period believe that society has collectively eschewed modern ideals and instead adopted ideas that are rooted in the reaction to the restrictions and limitations of those ideas, and that the present is therefore a new historical period. While the characteristics of postmodern life are sometimes difficult to grasp, most postmodern scholars point to concrete and visible technological and economic changes that they claim have brought about the new types of thinking.

Critics of the idea claim that it does not represent liberation, but rather a failure of creativity, and the supplanting of organisation with syncretism and bricolage; this latter concept can only be described as anti-intellectual. They argue that postmodernism is obscurantist, overly dense, and makes assertions about the sciences that are demonstrably false. There is a great deal of disagreement over whether or not recent technological and cultural changes represent a new historical period, or merely an extension of the modern one. Complicating matters further, others have argued that even the postmodern era has already ended, with some commentators asserting culture has entered a post-postmodern period.

3.6.1. Deconstructivism and Deconstruction

Deconstruction is a term which is used to denote the application of postmodern ideas of criticism, or theory, to a "text" or "artifact", based on the architecture deconstructivism. A deconstruction is meant to undermine the frame of reference and assumptions that underpin the text or the artifact.

In its original use, a "deconstruction" is an important textual "occurrence" described and analysed by many postmodern authors and philosophers. They argue that aspects in the text itself would undermine its own authority or assumptions and that internal contradictions would erase boundaries or categories which the work relied on or asserted.

Poststructuralists beginning with Jacques Derrida, who coined the term, argued that the existence of deconstructions implied that there was no intrinsic essence to a text, merely the contrast of difference. This is analogous to the scientific idea that only the variations are real, that there is no established norm to a genetic population, or the idea that the difference in perception between black and white is the context. A deconstruction is created when the "deeper" substance of text opposes the text's more "superficial" form. This idea is not isolated to poststructuralists but is related to the idea of hermeneutics in literature; intellectuals as early as Plato asserted it and so did modern thinkers such as Leo Strauss.

Popularly, close textual analyses describing deconstruction within a text are often themselves called *deconstructions*. Derrida argued, however, that deconstruction is not a method or a tool but an occurrence within the text itself. Writings about deconstruction are therefore referred to in academic circles as *deconstructive readings*.

Deconstruction is far more important to postmodernism than its seemingly narrow focus on *text* might imply. According to Derrida, one consequence of deconstruction is that the text may be defined so broadly as to encompass not just written words but the entire spectrum of symbols and phenomena within Western thought. To Derrida, a result of deconstruction is that no Western philosopher has been able to escape successfully from this large web of text and reach that which is "signified", which they imagined to exist "just beyond" the text.

3.6.1.1. Social construction, structuralism, poststructuralism

Often opposed to deconstruction are social constructionists, labelled as such within the analytic tradition, but not usually in the case of the continental tradition. The term was first used in sociologists Peter Berger and Thomas Luckmann's book *The Social Construction of Reality*. Usually in the continental tradition, the terms structuralism or poststructuralism are used. Maurice Merleau-Ponty is seen as the biggest contributor to structuralism, which is epitomised in the philosophy of Claude Levi-Strauss.

Michel Foucault was also a structuralist but then turned to what would be termed poststructuralism, although he himself declined to call his work either poststructuralist or postmodern.

Structuralism historically gave way to poststructuralism; often the role of postmodernism within the analytic tradition is played down, although works by major figures of the analytic tradition in the 20th century, including those of Thomas Kuhn and Willard Van Orman Quine, show a similarity with works in the continental tradition for their lack of belief in absolute [truth] as well as in the pliability of language. In the continental tradition, most works argue that power dissimulates and that society constructs reality, while its individuals remain powerless or almost powerless. Often, both continental and analytic sources argue for a renewed subjectivity, borrowing heavily from Immanuel Kant, while they largely reject his a priori/a posteriori distinction. They both minimise discussions of practical ethics, instead borrowing heavily from post-Holocaust accounts of the need for an ethics of responsibility, which is very rarely practically defined. One of the large differences between analytic postmodern sources and continental postmodern sources is that the analytic tradition by and large guards at least some of the tenets of liberalism, while many continental sources flirt with, or completely immerse themselves in, Marxism.

References

Backler, A., & Hanvey R., *Global geography,* NY: Teachers College Press, 1986.

_______________ ., & Stoltman, J., *A teacher's guide to global geography,* Bloomington, IN: Agency for Instructional Technology, 1988.

Caesar, Terry, "Motherhood and postmodernism", *American Literary History,* 1995.

Chouinard, Vera, "Structure and agency: Contested concepts in Human Geography", in C. Earle, K. Matthewson, and M.S. Kenzer, eds., *Concepts in Human Geography,* Lanham, MD: Rowman and Littlefield, 1997.

4

Economic Geography

Economic geography is the study of the location, distribution and spatial organisation of economic activities across the Earth. It focuses on the location of industries and retail and wholesale businesses, on transportation and trade, and on the changing value of real estate. Courses in economic geography may cover such topics as transportation, agriculture, industrial location, world trade, and the spatial organisation and function of business activity. Geology can affect resource availability, geomorphology, the cost of transportation, and the quality of soiled land alter economic activities. Climate can influence natural resource availability (forestry products) and location or type of agriculture. The social and political factors that are unique to a particular region also have an impact on economic decisions and further distributions of these activities.

Economic geography research focuses on the study of spatial aspects of economic activities on various scales. The distance to the city as a marketplace with demand for products plays a significant role in economic decisions of firms while other factors such as access to the sea and the presence of raw materials like oil affects the economic conditions of countries. Singapore, for example, occupies a key position as a seaport, while the wealth of Saudi Arabia depends almost entirely on oil.

4.1. History of Economic Geography

In the history of economic geography there were many influences coming mainly from economics and geographical sciences. First traces of the study of spatial aspects of economic activities on Earth can be found in Strabo's Geographika written almost 2000 years ago. During the period known in geography as environmental determinism notable influence came from Ellsworth Huntington and his theory of climatic determinism.

4.1.1. Environmental Determinism

Environmental determinism, also known as climatic determinism or geographical determinism, is the view that the physical environment, rather than social conditions, determines culture. Those who believe this view say that humans are strictly defined by stimulus-response (environment-behaviour) and cannot deviate.

Environmental determinism's origins go back to antiquity, when the Greek geographer Strabo wrote that climate influences the psychological disposition of different races. Similar ideas continued to be propounded up into the modern era.

Environmental determinism rose to prominence in the late 19th century and early 20th century when it was taken up as a central theory by the discipline of geography (and to a lesser extent, anthropology). Clark University professor Ellen Churchill Semple is credited with introducing the theory to the United States after studying with human geographer Friedrich Ratzel in Germany. The prominence of determinism was influenced by the high profile of evolutionary biology, although it tended more to resemble the now-discredited Lamarckism rather than Darwinism.

The fundamental argument of the environmental determinists was that aspects of physical geography, particularly that of climate, influenced the psychological mind-set of individuals, which in turn defined the behaviour and culture of the society that those individuals formed. For example, tropical climates were said to cause laziness, relaxed attitudes and promiscuity, while the frequent variability in the weather of the middle latitudes led to more determined and driven work ethics. Because these environmental influences operate slowly on human biology, it was important to trace the migrations of groups to see what environmental conditions they had evolved under.

Between 1920 and 1940, environmental determinism came under repeated attacks as its claims were found to be severely faulted at best, and often dangerously wrong. Geographers reacted to this by first developing the softer notion of "environmental possibilism," and later by abandoning the search for theory and causal explanation for many decades. Later critics charged that determinism served to justify racism and imperialism. The experience of environmental determinism has left a scar on geography, with many geographers reacting negatively to any suggestion of environmental influences on human society.

A variant of environmental determinism was popular among Marxists. To Marx's basic model of the ideological and cultural superstructure being determined by the economic base, they added the idea that the economic base is determined by environmental conditions. For example, Russian geographer Georgi Plekhanov argued that the reason his nation was still in the feudal era, rather than having progressed to capitalism and becoming ripe for the revolution into communism, was that the wide plains of Russia allowed class conflicts to be easily diffused. This Marxist environmental determinism was repudiated around the same time as classic environmental determinism.

4.1.2. Climatic Determinism

Climatic determinism or environmental determinism is an aspect of economic geography. Also sometimes called the equatorial paradox. According to this theory, about 70% of the economic development of a country can be predicted from the distance between that country and the equator. In other words, the further from the equator the more developed a country tends to be. The paradox applies equally well both north and south of the equator. Australia, for example, has a higher level of economic development than Indonesia. The paradox also applies within countries—the northern U.S. states are more developed than the southern U.S. states.

It is noteworthy that the equatorial paradox only emerged from the Modern Era onwards, with more highly developed cultures and economies being present in the tropical and subtropical regions than outside it. In the context of a statistical analysis, the paradox is probably more a consequence of subjugation and colonisation. The latter all but arrested economical and infrastructural development, except as needed to fulfil the colonial power's aims.

Location theory is concerned with the geographic location of economic activity; it has become an integral part of economic geography, regional science, and spatial economics. Location theory addresses the questions of what economic activities are located where and why. Location theory rests—like microeconomic theory generally—on the assumption that agents act in their own self interest. Thus firms choose locations that maximise their profits and individuals choose locations that maximise their utility.

4.2. Spatial Analysis

In statistics, spatial analysis or spatial statistics includes any of the formal techniques which study entities using their topological, geometric, or geographic properties. The phrase properly refers to a variety of techniques, many still in their early development, using different analytic approaches and applied in fields as diverse as astronomy, with its studies of the placement of galaxies in the cosmos, to chip fabrication engineering, with its use of 'place and route' algorithms to build complex wiring structures. The phrase is often used in a more restricted sense to describe techniques applied to structures at the human scale, most notably in the analysis of geographic data. The phrase is even sometimes used to refer to a specific technique in a single area of research, for example, to describe geostatistics.

The history of spatial analysis starts with early mapping, surveying and geography at the beginning of history, although the techniques of spatial analysis were not formalised until the later part of the twentieth century. Modern spatial analysis focuses on computer based techniques because of the large amount of data, the power of modern statistical and geographic information science (GIS) software, and the complexity of the computational modeling. Spatial analytic techniques have been developed in geography, biology, epidemiology, statistics, geographic information science, remote sensing, computer science, mathematics, and scientific modelling.

Complex issues arise in spatial analysis, many of which are neither clearly defined nor completely resolved, but form the basis for current research. The most fundamental of these is the problem of defining the spatial location of the entities being studied. For example, a study on human health could describe the spatial position of humans with a point placed where they live, or with a point located where they work, or by using a line to describe their weekly trips; each choice has dramatic effects on the techniques which can be used for the analysis and on the conclusions which can be obtained. Other issues in spatial analysis include the limitations of mathematical knowledge, the assumptions required by existing statistical techniques, and problems in computer based calculations.

4.2.1. History of spatial analysis

Spatial analysis can perhaps be considered to have arisen with the early attempts at cartography and surveying but many fields have contributed to its rise in modern form. Biology contributed through botanical studies of global plant distributions and local plant locations, ethological studies of animal movement, landscape ecological studies of vegetation blocks, ecological studies of spatial population dynamics, and the study of biogeography. Epidemiology contributed with early work on disease mapping, notably John Snow's work mapping an outbreak of cholera, with research on mapping the spread of disease and with locational studies for health care delivery. Statistics has contributed greatly through work in spatial statistics. Economics has contributed notably through spatial econometrics. Geographic information science is currently a major contributor due to the importance of geospatial software in the modern analytic toolbox. Remote sensing has contributed extensively in morphometric and clustering analysis. Computer science has contributed extensively through the study of algorithms, notably in computational geometry. Mathematics continues to provide the fundamental tools for analysis and to reveal the complexity of the spatial realm, for example, with recent work on fractals and scale invariance. Scientific modelling provides a useful framework for new approaches.

4.2.2. Fundamental Issues in Spatial Analysis

Spatial analysis confronts many fundamental issues in the definition of its objects of study, in the construction of the analytic operations to be used, in the use of computers for analysis, in the limitations and particularities of the analyses which are known, and in the presentation of analytic results. Many of these issues are active subjects of modern research.

Common errors often arise in spatial analysis, some due to the mathematics of space, some due to the particular ways data are presented spatially, some due to the tools which are available. Census data, because it protects individual privacy by aggregating data into local units, raises a number of statistical issues. Computer software can easily calculate the lengths of the lines which it defines but these may have no inherent meaning in the real world, as was shown for the coastline of Britain.

These problems represent one of the greatest dangers in spatial analysis because of the inherent power of maps as media of presentation. When results are presented as maps, the presentation combines the spatial data which is generally very accurate with analytic results which may be grossly inaccurate.

4.2.2.1. Spatial characterisation

The definition of the spatial presence of an entity constrains the possible analyses which can be applied to that entity and influences the final conclusions that can be reached. While this property is fundamentally true of all analysis, it is particularly important in spatial analysis because the tools to define and study entities favour specific characterisations of the entities being studied. Statistical techniques favour the spatial definition of objects as points because there are very few statistical techniques which operate directly on line, area, or volume elements. Computer tools favour the spatial definition of objects as homogeneous and separate elements because of the primitive nature of the computational structures available and the ease with which these primitive structures can be created.

There may also be arbitrary effects introduced by the spatial bounds or limits placed on the phenomenon or study area. This occurs since spatial phenomena may be unbounded or have ambiguous transition zones. This creates edge effects from ignoring spatial dependency or interaction outside the study area. It also imposes artificial shapes on the study area that can affect apparent spatial patterns such as the degree of clustering. A possible solution is similar to the sensitivity analysis strategy for the modifiable areal unit problem, or MAUP: change the limits of the study area and compare the results of the analysis under each realisation. Another possible solution is to overbound the study area. It is also feasible to eliminate edge effects in spatial modeling and simulation by mapping the region to a boundless object such as a torus or sphere.

4.2.2.2. Spatial dependency or auto-correlation

A fundamental concept in geography is that nearby entities often share more similarities than entities which are far apart. This idea is often labelled 'Tobler's first law of geography' and may be summarised as "everything is related to everything else, but nearby objects are more related than distant objects".

Spatial dependency is the co-variation of properties within a geo-space: characteristics at proximal locations appear to be correlated, either positively or negatively. There are at least three possible explanations. One possibility is there is a simple spatial correlation relationship: whatever is causing an observation in one location also causes similar observations in nearby locations. For example, physical crime rates in nearby areas within a city tend to be similar due to factors such as socio-economic status, amount of policing and the built environment creating the opportunities for that kind of crime: the features that attract one criminal will also attract others. Another possibility is spatial causality: something at a given location directly influences it in nearby locations. For example, the broken window theory of personal crime suggests that poverty, lack of maintenance and petty physical crime tends to breed more crime of this kind due to the apparent breakdown in order. A third possibility is spatial interaction: the movement of people, goods or information creates apparent relationships between locations. The "journey to crime" theory suggests that criminal activity occurs as a result of accessibility to a criminal's home, hangout or other key locations in his or her daily activities.

Spatial dependency leads to the spatial autocorrelation problem in statistics since, like temporal autocorrelation, this violates standard statistical techniques that assume independence among observations. For example, regression analyses that do not compensate for spatial dependency can have unstable parameter estimates and yield unreliable significance tests. Spatial regression models capture these relationships and do not suffer from these weaknesses. It is also appropriate to view spatial dependency as a source of information rather than something to be corrected.

Locational effects also manifest as spatial heterogeneity, or the apparent variation in a process with respect to location in a geospace. Unless a space is uniform and boundless, every location will have some degree of uniqueness relative to the other locations. This affects the spatial dependency relations and therefore the spatial process. Spatial heterogeneity means that overall parameters estimated for the entire system may not adequately describe the process at any given location.

4.2.2.3. Scaling

Spatial scale is a persistent issue in spatial analysis. The more fundamental issue of scale requires ensuring that the conclusion of the analysis does not depend on any arbitrary scale. Landscape ecologists failed to do this for many years and for a long time characterised landscape elements with quantitative metrics which depended on the scale at which they were measured. They eventually developed a series of scale invariant metrics.

4.2.3. Common Errors in Spatial Analysis

The fundamental issues in spatial analysis lead to numerous problems in analysis including bias, distortion and outright errors in the conclusions reached. These issues are often interlinked but various attempts have been made to separate out particular issues from each other.

4.2.3.1. Locational fallacy

The locational fallacy is a phrase used to describe an error due to the particular spatial characterisation chosen for the elements of study, in particular choice of placement for the spatial presence of the element.

Spatial characterisations may be simplistic or even wrong. Studies of humans often reduce the spatial existence of humans to a single point, for instance their home address. This can easily lead to poor analysis, for example, when considering disease transmission which can happen at work or at school and therefore far from the home.

The spatial characterisation may implicitly limit the subject of study. For example, the spatial analysis of 'crime' data has recently become popular but these studies can only describe the particular kinds of crime which can be described spatially. This leads to many maps of assault but not to any maps of embezzlement with political consequences in the conceptualisation of crime and the design of policies to address the issue.

4.2.3.2. Ecological Fallacy

The ecological fallacy describes errors due to performing analyses on aggregate data when trying to reach conclusions on the individual units. It is closely related to the Modifiable Areal Unit Problem.

4.2.3.3. Modifiable Areal Unit Problem

The modifiable areal unit problem (MAUP) is an issue in the analysis of spatial data arranged in zones, where the conclusion depends on the particular shape of the zones used in the analysis.

The problem arises because it is known that results derived an analysis of these zones depends directly on the zones being studied. It has been shown that the aggregation of point data into zones of different shape can lead to opposite conclusions. Various solutions have been proposed to address the MAUP, including repeated analysis and graphical techniques but the issue cannot yet be considered to be solved. One strategy is to assess its effects in a sensitivity analysis by changing the aggregation or boundaries and comparing results from the analysis and modeling under these different schemes. A second strategy is to develop optimal spatial units for the analysis.

4.2.4. Solutions to the Fundamental Issues

4.2.4.1. Geo-space

A mathematical space exists whenever we have a set of observations and quantitative measures of their attributes. The distances between individuals within this space is a quantitative measure of their differences with respect to income and education. However, in spatial analysis we are concerned with specific types of mathematical spaces, namely, geo-spaces. A geo-space is one where the observations correspond to locations in a spatial measurement framework that captures their proximity in the real world. The locations in a spatial measurement framework often represent locations on the surface of the Earth, but this is not strictly necessary. A spatial measurement framework can also capture proximity with respect to, say, interstellar space or within a biological entity such as a liver. The Euclidean distance between locations often represent their proximity, although this is only one possibility. There are an infinite number of distances in addition to Euclidean that can support quantitative analysis. For example, "Manhattan" distances where movement is restricted to paths parallel to the axes can be more meaningful than Euclidean distances in urban settings. In addition to distances, other geographic relationships such as connectivity and direction can also influence the relationships among entities. It is also possible to compute minimal cost paths across a cost surface; for example, this can represent proximity among locations when travel must occur across rugged terrain.

4.2.4.2. Spatial autocorrelation

Spatial autocorrelation statistics measure and analyse the degree of dependency among observations in a geo-space. Classic spatial autocorrelation statistics compare the spatial weights to the covariance relationship at pairs of locations. Spatial autocorrelation that is more positive than expected from random indicate the clustering of similar values across geo-space, while significant negative spatial autocorrelation indicates that neighbouring values are more dissimilar than expected by chance, suggesting a spatial pattern similar to a chess board. The possibility of spatial heterogeneity suggests that the estimated degree of autocorrelation may vary significantly across geo-space. Local spatial autocorrelation statistics provide estimates disaggregated to the level of the spatial analysis units, allowing assessment of the dependency relationships across space.

4.2.4.3. Spatial interpolation

Spatial interpolation methods estimate the variables at unobserved locations in geo-space based on the values at observed locations. Basic methods include inverse distance weighting: this attenuates the variable with decreasing proximity from the observed location. Kriging is a more sophisticated method that interpolates across space according to a spatial lag relationship that has both systematic and random components. This can accommodate a wide range of spatial relationships for the hidden values between observed locations. Kriging provides optimal estimates given the hypothesised lag relationship, and error estimates can be mapped to determine if spatial patterns exist.

4.2.4.4. Spatial regression

Spatial regression methods capture spatial dependency in regression analysis, avoiding statistical problems such as unstable parameters and unreliable significance tests, as well as providing information on spatial relationships among the variables involved. Depending on the specific technique, spatial dependency can enter the regression model as relationships between the independent variables and the dependent, between the dependent variables and a spatial lag of itself, or in the error terms. Geographically weighted regression (GWR) is a local version of spatial regression that generates parameters disaggregated by the spatial units of analysis. This allows assessment of the spatial heterogeneity in the estimated relationships between the independent and dependent variables.

4.2.4.5. Spatial interaction

Spatial interaction or "gravity models" estimate the flow of people, material or information between locations in geo-space. Factors can include origin propulsive variables such as the number of commuters in residential areas, destination attractiveness variables such as the amount of office space in employment areas, and proximity relationships between the locations measured in terms such as driving distance or travel time. After specifying the functional forms of these relationships, the analyst can estimate model parameters using observed flow data and standard estimation techniques such as ordinary least squares or maximum likelihood. Competing destinations versions of spatial interaction models include the proximity among the destinations (or origins) in addition to the origin-destination proximity; this captures the effects of destination (origin) clustering on flows. Computational methods such as artificial neural networks can also estimate spatial interaction relationships among locations and can handle noisy and qualitative data.

4.2.4.6. *Simulation and modeling*

Spatial interaction models are aggregate and top-down: they specify an overall governing relationship for flow between locations. This characteristic is also shared by urban models such as those based on mathematical programming, flows among economic sectors, or bid-rent theory. An alternative modeling perspective is to represent the system at the highest possible level of disaggregation and study the bottom-up emergence of complex patterns and relationships from behaviour and interactions at the individual level.

Complex adaptive systems theory as applied to spatial analysis suggests that simple interactions among proximal entities can lead to intricate, persistent and functional spatial entities at aggregate levels. Two fundamentally spatial simulation methods are cellular automata and agent-based modeling. The former method imposes a fixed spatial framework such as grid cells and specifies rules that dictate the state of a cell based on the states of its neighbouring cells. As time progresses, spatial patterns emerge as cells change states based on their neighbours; this alters the conditions for future time periods.

Agent-based modeling uses software entities (agents) that have purposeful behaviour (goals) and can react, interact and modify their environment while seeking their objectives. Unlike the cells in cellular automata, agents can be mobile with respect to space. For example, one could model traffic flow and dynamics using agents representing individual vehicles that try to minimise travel time between specified origins and destinations. While pursuing minimal travel times, the agents must avoid collisions with other vehicles also seeking minimum their travel times. Cellular automata and agent-based modeling are divergent yet complimentary modeling strategies. They can be integrated into a common geographic automata system where some agents are fixed while others are mobile.

4.2.4.7. Geographic Information Science and Spatial analysis

Geographic information systems (GIS) and the underlying geographic information science that advances these technologies have a strong influence on spatial analysis. The increasing ability to capture and handle geo-spatial data means that spatial analysis is occurring within increasingly data-rich environments. Geo-spatial data capture systems include remotely sensed imagery, environmental monitoring systems such as intelligent transportation systems, and location-aware technologies: mobile devices that can report location in near-real time. GIS provide platforms for managing these data, computing spatial relationships such as distance, connectivity and directional relationships between spatial units, and visualising both the raw data and spatial analytic results within a cartographic context.

Geovisualisation (GVis) combines scientific visualisation with digital cartography to support the exploration and analysis of geo-spatial data and information, including the results of spatial analysis or simulation. GVis leverages the human orientation towards visual information processing in the exploration, analysis and communication of geographic data and information. In contrast with traditional cartography, GVis is typically three or four-dimensional and user-interactive.

Geographic knowledge discovery (GKD) is the human-centered process of applying efficient computational tools for exploring massive spatial databases. GKD includes geographic data mining, but also encompasses related activities such as data selection, data cleaning and pre-processing, and interpretation of results. GVis can also serve a central role in the GKD process. GKD is based on the premise that massive databases contain interesting (valid, novel, useful and understandable) patterns that standard analytical techniques cannot find. GKD can serve as a hypothesis-generating process for spatial analysis, producing tentative patterns and relationships that should be confirmed using spatial analytical techniques. Spatial Decision Support Systems (sDSS) take existing spatial data and use a variety of mathematical models to make projections into the future. This allows urban and regional planners to test intervention decisions prior to implementation

4.3. Geographic Information System

A geographic information system (GIS) is a system for capturing, storing, analysing and managing data and associated attributes which are spatially referenced to the earth. In the strictest sense, it is a computer system capable of integrating, storing, editing, analysing, sharing, and displaying geographically-referenced information. In a more generic sense, GIS is a tool that allows users to create interactive queries, analyse the spatial information, edit data, maps, and present the results of all these operations. Geographic information science is the science underlying the geographic concepts, applications and systems, taught in degree and GIS Certificate programs at many universities.

4.3.1. Techniques Used in GIS

4.3.1.1. Data creation

Modern GIS technologies use digital information, for which various digitised data creation methods are used. The most common method of data creation is digitisation, where a hard copy map or survey plan is transferred into a digital medium through the use of a computer-aided design (CAD) programme, and geo-referencing capabilities. With the wide availability of ortho-rectified imagery (both from satellite and aerial sources), heads-up digitising is becoming the main avenue through which geographic data is extracted. Heads-up digitising involves the tracing of geographic data directly on top of the aerial imagery instead of through the traditional method of tracing the geographic form on a separate digitising tablet.

4.3.1.2. Data representation

GIS data represents real world objects (roads, land use, elevation) with digital data. Real world objects can be divided into two abstractions: discrete objects (a house) and continuous fields (rain fall amount or elevation). There are two broad methods used to store data in a GIS for both abstractions: Raster and Vector.

Raster

Raster data type consists of rows and columns of cells where in each cell is stored a single value. Most often, raster data are images (raster images), but besides just colour, the value recorded for each cell may be a discrete value, such as land use, a continuous value, such as rainfall, or a null value if no data is available. While a raster cell stores a single value, it can be extended by using raster bands to represent RGB (red, green, blue) colours, colourmaps (a mapping between a thematic code and RGB value), or an extended attribute table with one row for each unique cell value. The resolution of the raster data set is its cell width in ground units.

Raster data is stored in various formats; from a standard file-based structure of TIF, JPEG, etc. to binary long object (BLOB) data stored directly in a relational database management system (RDBMS) similar to other vector-based feature classes.

Vector

Vector data type uses geometries such as points, lines (series of point coordinates), or polygons, also called areas (shapes bounded by lines), to represent objects. Vector features can be made to respect spatial integrity through the application of topology rules such as 'polygons must not overlap'. Vector data can also be used to represent continuously varying phenomena. Contour lines and triangulated irregular networks (TIN) are used to represent elevation or other continuously changing values. TINs record values at point locations, which are connected by lines to form an irregular mesh of triangles. The face of the triangles represent the terrain surface.

There are advantages and disadvantages to using a raster or vector data model to represent reality. Raster data sets record a value for all points in the area covered which may require more storage space than representing data in a vector format that can store data only where needed. Raster data also allows easy implementation of overlay operations, which are more difficult with vector data. Vector data can be displayed as vector graphics used on traditional maps, whereas raster data will appear as an image that may have a blocky appearance for object boundaries. Vector data can be easier to register, scale, and re-project. This can simplify combining vector layers from different sources. Vector data are more compatible with relational database environment. They can be part of a relational table as a normal column and processes using a multitude of operators.

4.3.1.3. Voxel

Selected GIS additionally support the voxel data model. A voxel is a volume element, representing a value on a regular grid in three dimensional space. This is analogous to a pixel, which represents 2D image data. Voxels can be interpolated from 3D point clouds (3D point vector data), or merged from 2D raster slices.

4.3.1.4. Non-spatial data

Additional non-spatial data can also be stored besides the spatial data represented by the coordinates of a vector geometry or the position of a raster cell. In vector data, the additional data are attributes of the object. For example, a forest inventory polygon may also have an identifier value and information about tree species. In raster data the cell value can store attribute information, but it can also be used as an identifier that can relate to records in another table.

4.3.1.5. Data capture

Data capture-entering information into the system-consumes much of the time of GIS practitioners. There are a variety of methods used to enter data into a GIS where it is stored in a digital format.

Existing data printed on paper or PET film maps can be digitised or scanned to produce digital data. A digitiser produces vector data as an operator traces points, lines, and polygon boundaries from a map. Scanning a map results in raster data that could be further processed to produce vector data. Survey data can be directly entered into a GIS from digital data collection systems on survey instruments. Positions from a Global Positioning System (GPS), another survey tool, can also be directly entered into a GIS.

Remotely sensed data also plays an important role in data collection and consist of sensors attached to a platform. Sensors include cameras, digital scanners and LIDAR, while platforms usually consist of aircraft and satellites.

Satellite remote sensing provides another important source of spatial data. Here satellites use different sensor packages to passively measure the reflectance from parts of the electromagnetic spectrum or radio waves that were sent out from an active sensor such as radar. Remote sensing collects raster data that can be further processed to identify objects and classes of interest, such as land cover.

When data is captured, the user should consider if the data should be captured with either a relative accuracy or absolute accuracy, since this could not only influence how information will be interpreted but also the cost of data capture. In addition to collecting and entering spatial data, attribute data is also entered into a GIS. For vector data, this includes additional information about the objects represented in the system.

After entering data into a GIS, the data usually requires editing, to remove errors, or further processing. For vector data it must be made "topologically correct" before it can be used for some advanced analysis. For example, in a road network, lines must connect with nodes at an intersection. Errors such as undershoots and overshoots must also be removed. For scanned maps, blemishes on the source map may need to be removed from the resulting raster. For example, a fleck of dirt might connect two lines that should not be connected.

4.3.2. Raster-to-Vector Translation

Data restructuring can be performed by a GIS to convert data into different formats. For example, a GIS may be used to convert a satellite image map to a vector structure by generating lines around all cells with the same classification, while determining the cell spatial relationships, such as adjacency or inclusion. More advanced data processing can occur with image processing, a technique developed in the late 1960s by NASA and the private sector to provide contrast enhancement, false colour rendering and a variety of other techniques including use of two dimensional Fourier transforms. Since digital data are collected and stored in various ways, the two data sources may not be entirely compatible. So a GIS must be able to convert geographic data from one structure to another.

4.3.2.1. Projections, coordinate systems and registration

A property ownership map and a soils map might show data at

different scales. Map information in a GIS must be manipulated so that it registers, or fits, with information gathered from other maps. Before the digital data can be analysed, they may have to undergo other manipulations-projection and coordinate conversions. The earth can be represented by various models, each of which may provide a different set of coordinates for any given point on the earth's surface. The simplest model is to assume the earth is a perfect sphere. As more measurements of the earth have accumulated, the models of the earth have become more sophisticated and more accurate. In fact, there are models that apply to different areas of the earth to provide increased accuracy.

Projection is a fundamental component of map making. A projection is a mathematical means of transferring information from a model of the Earth, which represents a three-dimensional curved surface, to a two-dimensional medium-paper or a computer screen. Different projections are used for different types of maps because each projection particularly suits certain uses. For example, a projection that accurately represents the shapes of the continents will distort their relative sizes. Since much of the information in a GIS comes from existing maps, a GIS uses the processing power of the computer to transform digital information, gathered from sources with different projections and/or different coordinate systems, to a common projection and coordinate system.

4.3.3. Spatial analysis with GIS

4.3.3.1. Data modeling

It is difficult to relate wetlands maps to rainfall amounts recorded at different points such as airports, television stations, and high schools. A GIS, however, can be used to depict two- and three-dimensional characteristics of the Earth's surface, subsurface, and atmosphere from information points. For example, a GIS can quickly generate a map with isopleth or contour lines that indicate differing amounts of rainfall.

Such a map can be thought of as a rainfall contour map. Many sophisticated methods can estimate the characteristics of surfaces from a limited number of point measurements. A two-dimensional contour map created from the surface modeling of rainfall point measurements may be overlaid and analysed with any other map in a GIS covering the same area.

Additionally, from a series of three-dimensional points, or digital elevation model, isopleth lines representing elevation contours can be generated, along with slope analysis, shaded relief, and other elevation products. Watersheds can be easily defined for any given reach, by computing all of the areas contiguous and uphill from any given point of interest. Similarly, an expected thalweg of where surface water would want to travel in intermittent and permanent streams can be computed from elevation data in the GIS.

4.3.3.2. Cartographic modeling

The term "cartographic modeling" was (probably) coined by Dana Tomlin in his PhD dissertation and later in his book which has the term in the title. Cartographic modeling refers to a process where several thematic layers of the same area are produced, processed, and analysed. Tomlin used raster layers, but the overlay method can be used more generally. Operations on map layers can be combined into algorithms, and eventually into simulation or optimisation models.

4.3.3.3. Map overlay

The combination of two separate spatial data sets (points, lines or polygons) to create a new output vector data set. These overlays are similar to mathematical Venn diagram overlays. A union overlay combines the geographic features and attribute tables of both inputs into a single new output. An intersect overlay defines the area where both inputs overlap and retains a set of attribute fields for each. A symmetric difference overlay defines an output area that includes the total area of both inputs except for the overlapping area.

Data extraction is a GIS process similar to vector overlay, though it can be used in either vector or raster data analysis. Rather than combining the properties and features of both data sets, data extraction involves using a "clip" or "mask" to extract the features of one data set that fall within the spatial extent of another data set.

In raster data analysis, the overlay of data sets is accomplished through a process known as "local operation on multiple rasters" or "map algebra," through a function that combines the values of each raster's matrix. This function may weigh some inputs more than others through use of an "index model" that reflects the influence of various factors upon a geographic phenomenon.

4.3.3.4. Automated cartography

Digital cartography and GIS both encode spatial relationships in structured formal representations. GIS is used in digital cartography modeling as a (semi)automated process of making maps, so called Automated Cartography. In practice, it can be a subset of a GIS, within which it is equivalent to the stage of visualisation, since in most cases not all of the GIS functionality is used. Cartographic products can be either in a digital or in a hardcopy format. Powerful analysis techniques with different data representation can produce high-quality maps within a short time period. The main problem in Automated Cartography is to use a single set of data to produce multiple products at a variety of scales, a technique known as Generalisation.

4.3.3.5. Geostatistics

Geostatistics is a point-pattern analysis that produces field predictions from data points. It is a way of looking at the statistitical properties of those special data. It is different from general applications of statistics because it employs the use of graph theory and matrix algebra to reduce the number of parameters in the data. Only the second-order properties of the GIS data are analysed.

When phenomena are measured, the observation methods dictate the accuracy of any subsequent analysis. Due to the nature of the data, a constant or dynamic degree of precision is always lost in the measurement. This loss of precision is determined from the scale and distribution of the data collection.

To determine the statistical relevance of the analysis, an average is determined so that points(gradients) outside of any immediate measurement can be included to determine their predicted behaviour. This is due to the limitations of the applied statistic and data collection methods, and interpolation is required in order to predict the behaviour of particles, points, and locations that are not directly measurable.

Interpolation is the process by which a surface is created, usually a raster data set, through the input of data collected at a number of sample points. There are several forms of interpolation, each which treats the data differently, depending on the properties of the data set. In comparing interpolation methods, the first consideration should be whether or not the source data will change. Next is whether the method is subjective, a human interpretation, or objective. Then there is the nature of transitions between points: are they abrupt or gradual. Finally, there is whether a method is global (it uses the entire data set to form the model), or local where an algorithm is repeated for a small section of terrain.

Interpolation is a justified measurement because of a Spatial Autocorrelation Principle that recognises that data collected at any position will have a great similarity to, or influence of those locations within its immediate vicinity.

4.3.3.6. Address geocoding

Geocoding is calculating spatial locations (X,Y coordinates) from street addresses. A reference theme is required to geocode individual addresses, such as a road centerline file with address ranges. The individual address locations are interpolated, or estimated, by examining address ranges along a road segment. These are usually provided in the form of a table or database. The GIS will then place a dot approximately where that address belongs along the segment of centerline. Geocoding can also be applied against actual parcel data, typically from municipal tax maps. In this case, the result of the geocoding will be an actually positioned space as opposed to an interpolated point.

Various algorithms are used to help with address matching when the spellings of addresses differ. Address information that a particular entity or organisation has data on, such as the post office, may not entirely match the reference theme. There could be variations in street name spelling, community name, etc. Consequently, the user generally has the ability to make matching criteria more stringent, or to relax those parameters so that more addresses will be mapped. Care must be taken to review the results so as not to erroneously map addresses incorrectly due to overzealous matching parameters.

4.3.3.7. Reverse geocoding

Reverse geocoding is the process of returning an estimated street address number as it relates to a given coordinate. For example, a user can click on a road centerline theme (thus providing a coordinate) and have information returned that reflects the estimated house number. This house number is interpolated from a range assigned to that road segment.

4.3.3.8. Data output and cartography

Cartography is the design and production of maps, or visual representations of spatial data. The vast majority of modern cartography is done with the help of computers, usually using a GIS. Most GIS software gives the user substantial control over the appearance of the data.

4.3.3.9. Graphic display techniques

Traditional maps are abstractions of the real world, a sampling of important elements portrayed on a sheet of paper with symbols to represent physical objects. People who use maps must interpret these symbols. Topographic maps show the shape of land surface with contour lines; the actual shape of the land can be seen only in the mind's eye.

Today, graphic display techniques such as shading based on altitude in a GIS can make relationships among map elements visible, heightening one's ability to extract and analyse information.

4.3.3.10. Spatial ETL

Spatial ETL tools provide the data processing functionality of traditional Extract, Transform, Load (ETL) software, but with a primary focus on the ability to manage spatial data. They provide GIS users with the ability to translate data between different standards and proprietary formats, whilst geometrically transforming the data en-route.

4.3.4. GIS software

Geographic information can be accessed, transferred, transformed, overlaid, processed and displayed using numerous software applications. Within industry commercial offerings from companies such as ESRI and Mapinfo dominate, offering an entire suite of tools. Government and military departments often use custom software, open source products, such as GRASS, or more specialised products that meet a well defined need. Although free tools exist to view GIS datasets, public access to geographic information is dominated by online resources such as Google Earth and interactive web mapping.

Originally up to the late 1990s, when GIS data was mostly based on large computers and used to maintain internal records, software was a stand-alone product. However with increased access to the internet and networks and demand for distributed geographic data grew, GIS software gradually changed its entire outlook to the delivery of data over a network. GIS software is now usually marketed as combination of various interoperable applications and API's.

4.3.4.1. Data creation

GIS processing software is used for the task preparing data for use within a GIS. This transforms the raw or legacy geographic data into a format usable by GIS products. This can be distinguished from the transformations done within GIS analysis software by the fact that these changes are permanent, more complex and time consuming. This a specialised high-end type of software is generally used by person skilled in photogrammetry and/or GIS processing aspects of computer science. In addition, AutoCAD, normally used for draughts of engineering projects, can be configured for the editing of vector maps, and has some products that have migrating towards GIS use. It is especially useful as it has strong support for digitisation. Raw geographic data can be edited in many standard database and spreadsheet applications and in some cases a text editor may be used as long as care is taken to properly format data.

4.3.5. Geodatabases

A geodatabase is a database with extensions for storing, querying, and manipulating geographic information and spatial data.

4.3.5.1. Management and analysis

GIS analysis software takes GIS data and overlays or otherwise combines it so that the data can be visually analysed. It can output a detailed map, image or movie used to communicate an idea or concept with respect to a region of interest. This is usually used by persons who are trained in cartography, geography or a GIS professional as this type of application is complex and takes some time to master. The software performs transformation on raster and vector data sometimes of differing datums, grid system, or reference system, into one coherent image. It can also analyse changes over time within a region.

4.3.5.2. Readers

GIS readers are computer applications that are designed to allow users to easily view digital maps as well as view and query GIS-managed data. By definition, they usually allow very little if any editing of the map or underlying map data. Readers can be normal standalone applications that need to be installed locally, though they are often designed to connect to data servers over the Internet to access the relevant information. Readers can also be included as an embedded application within a web page, obviating the need for local installation. Readers are designed to be relatively simple and easy to use as well as free.

4.3.5.3. Web API

This is the evolution of the scripts that were common with most early GIS systems. An application programming interface is a set of subroutines designed to perform a specific task. GIS API's are designed to manage GIS data for its delivery to a web browser client from a GIS server. They are accessed with commonly used scripting language such as VBA or JavaScript. They are used to build a server system for the delivery of GIS that is to made available over an intranet or publicly over the Internet.

4.3.5.4. Mobile GIS

GIS has seen many implementations on mobile devices. With the widespread adoption of GPS, GIS has been used to capture and integrate data in the field.

4.3.5.5. Vehicle navigation

A database model of a network of roads and related features is a form of GIS data that is used for vehicle navigation systems. Such a map database is a vector representation of a given road network including road geometry (segment shape), network topology (connectivity) and related attributes (addresses, road class, etc). Geographic Data Files (GDF) is an ISO standard for formulating map databases for navigation. An Automotive navigation system will combine map-matching, GPS coordinates, and Dead reckoning to estimate the position of the vehicle. The map database is also used for route planning and guidance, and possibly advanced functions involving active safety, driver assistance and location-based services. Maintenance of databases for vehicle navigation is discussed in the article Map database management.

4.4. Future of GIS

Many disciplines can benefit from GIS technology. An active GIS market has resulted in lower costs and continual improvements in the hardware and software components of GIS. These developments will, in turn, result in a much wider use of the technology throughout science, government, business, and industry, with applications including real estate, public health, crime mapping, national defence, sustainable development, natural resources, landscape architecture, archaeology, regional and community planning, transportation and logistics. GIS is also diverging into location-based services (LBS). LBS allows GPS enabled mobile devices to display their location in relation to fixed assets (nearest restaurant, gas station, fire hydrant), mobile assets (friends, children, police car) or to relay their position back to a central server for display or other processing. These services continue to develop with the increased integration of GPS functionality with increasingly powerful mobile electronics (cell phones, PDA's, laptops).

4.4.1. Web Mapping

In recent years there has been an explosion of mapping applications on the web such as Google Maps, MapQuest, Yahoo! Maps, Rand McNally. These websites give the public access to huge amounts of geographic data with an emphasis on aerial photography. Some of them, like Google Maps, expose an API that enable users to create custom applications. These vendors' applications offer street maps and aerial/satellite imagery that support such features as geocoding, searches, and routing functionality.

Maps have traditionally been used to explore the Earth and to exploit its resources. GIS technology, as an expansion of cartographic science, has enhanced the efficiency and analytic power of traditional mapping. Now, as the scientific community recognises the environmental consequences of human activity, GIS technology is becoming an essential tool in the effort to understand the process of global change. Various map and satellite information sources can combine in modes that simulate the interactions of complex natural systems.

Through a function known as visualisation, a GIS can be used to produce images—not just maps, but drawings, animations, and other cartographic products. These images allow researchers to view their subjects in ways that literally never have been seen before. The images often are equally helpful in conveying the technical concepts of GIS study-subjects to non-scientists.

GIS technology and the availability of digital data on regional and global scales enable such analyses. The satellite sensor output used to generate a vegetation graphic is produced by the Advanced Very High Resolution Radiometer (AVHRR). This sensor system detects the amounts of energy reflected from the Earth's surface across various bands of the spectrum for surface areas of about 1 square kilometer. The satellite sensor produces images of a particular location on the Earth twice a day. AVHRR is only one of many sensor systems used for Earth surface analysis. More sensors will follow, generating ever greater amounts of data.

GIS and related technology will help greatly in the management and analysis of these large volumes of data, allowing for better understanding of terrestrial processes and better management of human activities to maintain world economic vitality and environmental quality.

In addition to the integration of time in environmental studies, GIS is also being explored for its ability to track and model the progress of humans throughout their daily routines. A concrete example of progress in this area is the recent release of time-specific population data by the US Census. In this data set, the populations of cities are shown for daytime and evening hours highlighting the pattern of concentration and dispersion generated by North American commuting patterns. The manipulation and generation of data required to produce this data would not have been possible without GIS. Using models to project the data held by a GIS forward in time have enabled planners to test policy decisions. These systems are known as Spatial Decision Support Systems.

4.4.2. Semantics and GIS

Tools and technologies emerging from the W3C's Semantic Web Activity are proving useful for data integration problems in information systems. Correspondingly, such technologies have been proposed as a means to facilitate interoperability and data reuse among GIS applications and also to enable new analysis mechanisms.

Ontologies are a key component of this semantic approach as they allow a formal, machine-readable specification of the concepts and relationships in a given domain. This in turn allows a GIS to focus on the meaning of data rather than its syntax or structure. Valuable contributions came from location theorists such as Johann Heinrich von Thünen or Alfred Weber. Other influential theories were Walter Christaller's Central place theory, the theory of core and periphery. Quantitative methods became prevailing in research.

4.5. Conclusion

Contemporary economic geographers tend to specialise in areas such as location theory and spatial analysis, market research, geography of transportation, land or real estate price evaluation, regional and global development, planning, Internet geography, and others.

Spatial analysis and modeling often involves aggregate spatial units such as census tracts and traffic analysis zones. These units may reflect data collection and/or modeling convenience rather than homogeneous, cohesive regions in the real world. The spatial units are therefore arbitrary or modifiable and contain artifacts related to the degree of spatial aggregation or the placement of boundaries.

In today's world location, distribution and character of economic activities is much influenced by globalisation. States and their borders play less significant role as many countries tend to eliminate the effects of borders and deepen the mutual cooperation on the global scale. Border regions that are often economically marginal and underdeveloped are also better cooperating with each other. The best example is the creation of European Union. Significant characteristics is also the occurrence of large business clusters that are forming around the world.

References

Davis, D.R., and Weinstein, D.E., "Economic geography and regional production structure: An empirical investigation", *European Economic Review,* Vol. 43, 1999.

________________ ., "Market Access, Economic Geographyand Comparative Advantage: An Empirical Assessment", *Journal of International Economics,* Vol. 2003.

Fujita M., "Urban Economic Theory: Land Use and City Size", Cambridge University Press, 1991.

________________ ., Henderson J.V., and Mori T.,"Spatial Distribution of Economic Activities in Japan and China", *Handbook of Regional and Urban Economics,* Vol.4. 2004.

Redding S., and A. Venables, "Economic Geography and International Inequality", *Journal of International Economics,* 2004.

5

Historical Geography

Historical geography is the study of the human, physical, fictional, theoretical, and "real" geographies of the past. Historical geography studies a wide variety of issues and topics. A common theme is the study of the geographies of the past and how a place or region changes through time. Many historical geographers study geographical patterns through time, including how people have interacted with their environment, and created the cultural landscape. Historical geography seeks to determine how cultural features of various societies across the planet emerged and evolved, by understanding their interaction with their local environment and surroundings.

A landscape and the cultures in it could only be understood if all of its influences through history were taken into account: physical, cultural, economic, political, environmental. Regional specialisation is the only means of gaining sufficient expertise on regions of the world. Sauer's philosophy was the principal shaper of American geographic thought in the mid-20th century. Regional specialists remain in academic geography departments to this day. But some geographers feel that it harmed the discipline; that too much effort was spent on data collection and classification, and too little on analysis and explanation. Studies became more and more area-specific as later geographers struggled to find places to make names for themselves.

5.1. Physical Geography: Geographies of Places and Environments

Physical geography is one of the two major subfields of geography. Physical geography focuses on understanding the processes and patterns in the natural environment, as opposed to the built environment which is the domain of Human geography. Within the body of physical geography the Earth is often split either into several spheres or into different environments, with the main spheres being the; Atmosphere, Biosphere, Cryosphere, Geosphere, Hydrosphere, Lithosphere and Pedosphere. Within physical geography there are various fields of study, mainly but not exclusively focusing on the spheres of the earth. Research in physical geography is often interdisciplinary and uses the systems approach.

5.1.1. Geomorphology

Geomorphology is the study of landforms, including their origin and evolution, and the processes that shape them. Geomorphologists seek to understand landform history and dynamics, and predict future changes through a combination of field observation, physical experiment, and numerical modeling. The discipline is practiced within geology, geodesy, geography, archaeology, and civil and environmental engineering. Early studies in geomorphology are the foundation for pedology, one of two main branches of soil science.

Perhaps the earliest one to devise a theory of geomorphology was the polymath Chinese scientist and statesman Shen Kuo. This was based on his observation of marine fossil shells in a geological stratum of a mountain hundreds of miles from the Pacific Ocean. Noticing bivalve shells running in a horizontal span along the cut section of a cliffside, he theorised that the cliff was once the pre-historic location of a seashore that had shifted hundreds of miles over the centuries. He inferred that the land was reshaped and formed by soil erosion of the mountains and by deposition of silt, after observing strange natural erosions of the Taihang Mountains and the Yandang Mountain near Wenzhou. Furthermore, he promoted the theory of gradual climate change over centuries of time once ancient petrified bamboos were found to be preserved underground in the dry, northern climate zone of Yanzhou, which is now modern day Yan'an, Shaanxi province.

Geomorphology was not originally differentiated from the rest of geography. The first geomorphic model was the geographical cycle or the cycle of erosion, developed by William Morris Davis between 1884 and 1899. The cycle was inspired by theories of uniformitarianism which were first formulated by James Hutton. Concerning valley forms, the cycle was depicted as a sequence by which a river would cut a valley more and more deeply, but then erosion of side valleys would eventually flatten out the terrain again, now at a lower elevation. The cycle could be started over by uplift of the terrain. The model is today considered too much of a simplification to be especially useful in practice.

Walther Penck developed an alternative model in the 1920s, based on ratios of uplift and erosion, but it was also too weak to explain a variety of landforms. G. K. Gilbert was an important early American geomorphologist.

Modern geomorphology focuses on the quantitative analysis of interconnected processes, such as the contribution of solar energy, the rates of steps of the hydrologic cycle, plate movement rates from geophysics to compute the age and expected fate of landforms and the weathering and erosion of the land. The use of more precise measurement technique has also enabled processes like erosion to be observed directly, rather than merely surmised from other evidence. Computer simulation is also valuable for testing that a particular model yields results with properties similar to real terrain. Primary surface processes responsible for most topographic features include wind, waves, weathering, mass wasting, ground water, surface water, glaciers, tectonism, and volcanism.

5.1.1.1. Fluvial geomorphology

Rivers and streams are not only conduits of water, but also of sediment. The water, as it flows over the channel bed, is able to mobilise sediment and transport it downstream, either as bedload, suspended load or dissolved load. The rate of sediment transport depends on the availability of sediment itself and on the river's discharge.

As rivers flow across the landscape, they generally increase in size, merging with other rivers. The network of rivers thus formed is a drainage system and is often dendritic, but may adopt other patterns depending on the regional topography and underlying geology.

5.1.1.2. Glacial geomorphology

Glaciers, while geographically restricted, are effective agents of landscape change. The gradual movement of ice down a valley causes abrasion and plucking of the underlying rock. Abrasion produces fine sediment, termed glacial flour. The debris transported by the glacier, when the glacier recedes, is termed a moraine. Glacial erosion is responsible for U-shaped valleys, as opposed to the V-shaped valleys of fluvial origin.

Weathering

This results from chemical dissolution of rock and from the mechanical wearing of rock by plant roots, ice expansion, and the abrasive action of sediment. Weathering provides the source of the sediment transported by fluvial, glacial, aeolian, or biotic processes.

5.1.1.3. Hydrology

Hydrology is the study of the movement, distribution, and quality of water throughout the Earth, and thus addresses both the hydrologic cycle and water resources. A practitioner of hydrology is a hydrologist, working within the fields of either earth or environmental science, physical geography or civil and environmental engineering. Domains of hydrology include hydrometeorology, surface hydrology, hydrogeology, drainage basin management and water quality, where water plays the central role. Oceanography and meteorology are not included because water is only one of many important aspects.

Hydrologic cycle

The central theme of hydrology is that water moves throughout the Earth through different pathways and at different rates. The most vivid image of this is in the evaporation of water from the ocean, which forms clouds. These clouds drift over the land and produce rain. The rainwater flows into lakes, rivers, or aquifers. The water in lakes, rivers, and aquifers then either evaporates back to the atmosphere or eventually flows back to the ocean, completing a cycle.

Hydrologic measurements

The movement of water through the Earth can be measured in a number of ways. This information is important for both assessing water resources and understanding the processes involved in the hydrologic cycle.

Hydrologic prediction

Observations of hydrologic processes are used to make predictions of the future behaviour of hydrologic systems (water flow, water quality). One of the major current concerns in hydrologic research is the Prediction in Ungauged Basins (PUB), i.e. in basins where no or only very few data exist.

Statistical hydrology

By analysing the statistical properties of hydrologic records, such as rainfall or river flow, hydrologists can estimate future hydrologic phenomena. This, however, assumes the characteristics of the processes remain unchanged. These estimates are important for engineers and economists so that proper risk analysis can be performed to influence investment decisions in future infrastructure and to determine the yield reliability characteristics of water supply systems. Statistical information is utilised to formulate operating rules for large dams forming part of systems which include agricultural, industrial and residential demands.

Hydrologic modeling

Hydrologic models are simplified, conceptual representations of a part of the hydrologic cycle. They are primarily used for hydrologic prediction and for understanding hydrologic processes. Recent research in hydrologic modeling tries to have a more global approach to the understanding of the behaviour of hydrologic systems to make better predictions and to face the major challenges in water resources management.

Hydrologic transport

Water movement is a significant means by which other material, such as soil or pollutants, are transported from place to place.

Initial input to receiving waters may arise from a point source discharge or a line source or area source, such as surface runoff. Since the 1960s rather complex mathematical models have been developed, facilitated by the availability of high speed computers. The most common pollutant classes analysed are nutrients, pesticides, total dissolved solids and sediment.

5.2. Biogeography: Geography of Species Distribution and the Process

Biogeography is the science which deals with geographic patterns of species distribution and the processes that result in such patterns. The patterns of species distribution at this level can usually be explained through a combination of historical factors such as speciation, extinction, continental drift, glaciation (and associated variations in sea level, river routes, and so on), and river capture, in combination with the area and isolation of landmasses (geographic constraints) and available energy supplies.

The theory of biogeography grows out of the work of Alfred Russel Wallace and other early evolutionary scientists. Wallace studied the distribution of flora and fauna in the Malay Archipelago in the 19th century. With the exception of Wallace and a few others, prior to the publication of The Theory of Island Biogeography by Robert MacArthur and E.O. Wilson in 1967 the field of biogeography was seen as a primarily historical one, and as such the field was seen as a purely descriptive one.

MacArthur and Wilson changed this perception, and showed that the species richness of an area could be predicted in terms of such factors as habitat area, immigration rate and extinction rate. This gave rise to an interest in island biogeography. The application of island biogeography theory to habitat fragments spurred the development of the fields of conservation biology and landscape ecology.

Classic biogeography has been expanded by the development of molecular systematics, creating a new discipline known as phylogeography. This development allowed scientists to test theories about the origin and dispersal of populations, such as island endemics. For example, while classic biogeographers were able to speculate about the origins of species in the Hawaiian

Islands, phylogeography allows them to test theories of relatedness between these populations and putative source populations in Asia and North America.

Paleobiogeography goes one step further to include paleogeographic data and considerations of plate tectonics. Using molecular analyses and corroborated by fossils, it has been possible to demonstrate that perching birds evolved first in the region of Australia or the adjacent Antarctic. From there, they spread to the other Gondwanan continents and Southeast Asia - the part of Laurasia then closest to their origin of dispersal - in the late Paleogene, before achieving a global distribution in the early Neogene. Not knowing the fact that at the time of dispersal, the Indian Ocean was much narrower than it is today, and that South America was closer to the Antarctic, one would be hard pressed to explain the presence of many "ancient" lineages of perching birds in Africa, as well as the mainly South American distribution of the suboscines.

Biogeography is a synthetic science, related to geography, biology, soil science, geology, climatology, ecology and evolution.

5.2.1. Climatology

5.2.1.1. Climate indices

Scientists use climate indices in their attempt to characterise and understand the various climate mechanisms that culminate in our daily weather. Much in the way the Dow Jones Industrial Average, which is based on the stock prices of 30 companies, is used to represent the fluctuations in the stock market as a whole, climate indices are used to represent the essential elements of climate. Climate indices are generally devised with the twin objectives of simplicity and completeness, and each index typically represents the status and timing of the climate factor it represents. By their very nature, indices are simple, and combine many details into a generalised, overall description of the atmosphere or ocean which can be used to characterise the factors which impact the global climate system.

Southern Oscillation

Southern Oscillation (ENSO) is a global coupled ocean-atmosphere phenomenon. The Pacific ocean signatures, El Niño and La Niña are important temperature fluctuations in surface waters of the tropical Eastern Pacific Ocean. The name El Niño, from the Spanish for "the little boy", refers to the Christ child, because the phenomenon is usually noticed around Christmas time in the Pacific Ocean off the west coast of South America. La Niña means "the little girl." Their effect on climate in the subtropics and the tropics are profound. The atmospheric signature, the Southern Oscillation (SO) reflects the monthly or seasonal fluctuations in the air pressure difference between Tahiti and Darwin. The most recent occurrence of El Niño started in September 2006 and lasted until early 2007.

ENSO is a set of interacting parts of a single global system of coupled ocean-atmosphere climate fluctuations that come about as a consequence of oceanic and atmospheric circulation. ENSO is the most prominent known source of inter-annual variability in weather and climate around the world, though not all areas are affected. ENSO has signatures in the Pacific, Atlantic and Indian Oceans. El Niño causes weather patterns which causes it to rain in specific places but not in others, this is one of many causes for the drought. In the Pacific, during major warm events, El Niño warming extends over much of the tropical Pacific and becomes clearly linked to the SO intensity. While ENSO events are basically in phase between the Pacific and Indian Oceans, ENSO events in the Atlantic Ocean lag behind those in the Pacific by 12 to 18 months.

Madden-Julian Oscillation

The Madden-Julian Oscillation (MJO) is an equatorial travelling pattern of anomalous rainfall that is planetary in scale. It is characterised by an eastward progression of large regions of both enhanced and suppressed tropical rainfall, observed mainly over the Indian Ocean and Pacific Ocean. The anomalous rainfall is usually first evident over the western Indian Ocean, and remains evident as it propagates over the very warm ocean waters of the western and central tropical Pacific. This pattern of tropical rainfall then generally becomes very nondescript as it moves over the cooler ocean waters of the eastern Pacific but reappears over the tropical Atlantic and Indian Ocean. The wet phase of enhanced convection and precipitation is followed by a dry phase where convection is suppressed.

North Atlantic Oscillation (NAO)

Indices of the NAO are based on the difference of normalised sea level pressure (SLP) between Ponta Delgada, Azores and Stykkisholmur/Reykjavik, Iceland. The SLP anomalies at each station were normalised by division of each seasonal mean pressure by the long-term mean standard deviation. Normalisation is done to avoid the series of being dominated by the greater variability of the northern of the two stations. Positive values of the index indicate stronger-than-average westerlies over the middle latitudes.

Pacific Decadal Oscillation (PDO)

The PDO is a pattern of Pacific climate variability that shifts phases on at least inter-decadal time scale, usually about 20 to 30 years. The PDO is detected as warm or cool surface waters in the Pacific Ocean, north of 20° N. During a "warm", or "positive", phase, the west Pacific becomes cool and part of the eastern ocean warms; during a "cool" or "negative" phase, the opposite pattern occurs. The mechanism by which the pattern lasts over several years has not been identified; one suggestion is that a thin layer of warm water during summer may shield deeper cold waters. A PDO signal has been reconstructed to 1661 through tree-ring chronologies in the Baja California area.

Interdecadal Pacific Oscillation (IPO)

The Interdecadal Pacific Oscillation (IPO or ID) display similar sea surface temperature (SST) and sea level pressure patterns to the PDO, with a cycle of 15-30 years, but affects both the north and south Pacific. In the tropical Pacific, maximum SST anomalies are found away from the equator. This is quite different to the quasi-decadal oscillation (QDO) with a period of 8-to-12 years and maximum SST anomalies straddling the equator, thus resembling ENSO.

*5.2.1.2. **Climate models***

Climate models use quantitative methods to simulate the

interactions of the atmosphere, oceans, land surface, and ice. They are used for a variety of purposes from study of the dynamics of the weather and climate system to projections of future climate. All climate models balance, or very nearly balance, incoming energy as short wave electromagnetic radiation to the earth with outgoing energy as long wave (infrared) electromagnetic radiation from the earth. Any unbalance results in a change in the average temperature of the earth. The most talked-about models of recent years have been those relating temperature to emissions of carbon dioxide. These models predict an upward trend in the surface temperature record, as well as a more rapid increase in temperature at higher altitudes.

5.2.2. Pedology

Pedology is the study of soils in its natural environment. It is one of two main branches of soil science, the other being edaphology. Pedology deals with pedogenesis, soil morphology, soil classification.

Soil is not only a support for vegetation, but it is also the zone (the pedosphere) of numerous interactions between climate (water, air, temperature), soil life (micro-organisms, plants, animals) and its residues, the mineral material of the original and added rock, and its position in the landscape. During its formation and genesis, the soil profile slowly deepens and develops characteristic layers, called 'horizons', while a steady state balance is approached.

Soil users (such as agronomists) showed initially little concern in the dynamics of soil. They saw it as medium whose chemical, physical and biological properties were useful for the services of agronomic productivity. On the other hand, pedologists and geologists did not initially focus on the agronomic applications of the soil characteristics (edaphic properties) but upon its relation to the nature and history of landscapes.

Pedologists are now also interested in the practical applications of a good understanding of pedogenesis processes (the evolution and functioning of soils), like interpreting its environmental history and predicting consequences of changes in land use, while agronomists understand that the cultivated soil is a complex medium, often resulting from several thousands of years of evolution. They understand that the current balance is fragile and that only a thorough knowledge of its history makes it possible to ensure its sustainable use.

5.2.3. High-energy Coastline

5.2.3.1. Coastal geography

Coastal geography is the study of the dynamic interface between the ocean and the land, incorporating both the physical geography (i.e coastal geomorphology, geology and oceanography) and the human geography (sociology and history) of the coast. It involves an understanding of coastal weathering processes, particularly wave action, sediment movement and weather, and also the ways in which humans interact with the coast.

5.2.3.2. Wave action and longshore dift

The waves of different strengths that constantly hit against the shoreline are the primary movers and shapers of the coastline. Despite the simplicity of this process, the differences between waves and the rocks they hit result in hugely varying shapes. The effect that waves have depends on their strength. Strong, also called destructive waves occur on high energy beaches and are typical of Winter. They reduce the quantity of sediment present on the beach by carrying it out to bars under the sea. Constructive, weak waves are typical of low energy beaches and occur most during summer. They do the opposite to destructive waves and increase the size of the beach by piling sediment up onto the berm.

One of the most important transport mechanisms results from wave refraction. Since waves rarely break onto a shore at right angles, the upward movement of water onto the beach (swash) occurs at an oblique angle. However, the return of water (backwash) is at right angles to the beach, resulting in the net movement of beach material laterally. This movement is known as beach drift. The endless cycle of swash and backwash and resulting beach drift can be observed on all beaches.

Probably the most important effect is longshore drift (LSD), the process by which sediment is continuously moved along beaches by wave action. LSD occurs because waves hit the shore at an angle, pick up sediment (sand) on the shore and carry it down the beach at an angle (this is called swash). Due to gravity, the water then falls back perpendicular to the beach, dropping its sediment as it loses energy. The sediment is then picked up by the next wave and pushed slightly further down the beach, resulting in a continual movement of sediment in one direction. This is the reason why long strips of coast are covered in sediment, not just the areas around river mouths, which are the main sources of beach sediment. LSD is reliant on a constant supply of sediment from rivers and if sediment supply is stopped or sediment falls into a submarine canals at any point along a beach, this can lead to bare beaches further along the shore.

LSD helps create many landforms including barriers, bay beaches and spits. In general LSD action serves to straighten the coast because the creation of barriers cuts off bays from the sea while sediment usually builds up in bays because the waves there are weaker (due to wave refraction), while sediment is carried away from the exposed headlands. The lack of sediment on headlands removes the protection from waves them and makes them more vulnerable to weathering while the gathering of sediment in bays protects the bays from further erosion and makes them pleasant recreational beaches.

5.2.3.3. *Biological processes*

In tropical regions in particular, plants and animals not only affect the weathering of rocks but are a source of sediment themselves. The shells and skeletons of many organisms are of calcium carbonate and when this is broken down it forms sediment, limestone and clay.

5.2.3.4. *Physical processes*

The main Physical Weathering process on beaches is salt-crystal growth. Wind carries salt spray onto rocks, where it is absorbed into small pores and cracks within the rocks. There the water evaporates and the salt crystallises, creating pressure and often breaking down the rock. In some beaches calcium carbonate is able to bind together other sediments to form beachrock and in warmer areas dunerock.

5.2.3.5. *Sea level changes*

Because the sea level on earth regularly rises and falls due to climatic changes. During cold periods more of the Earth's water is stored as ice in glaciers while during warm periods it is released and sea levels rise to cover more land. Sea levels are currently quite high, while just 18,000 years ago during the Pleistocene ice age they were quite low. Global warming may result in further rises in the future, which presents a risk to coastal cities as most would be flooded by only small rises. As sea levels rise fjords and rias form. Fjords are flooded glacial valleys and rias are flooded river valleys. Fjords typically have steep rocky sides, while rias have dendritic drainage patterns typical of drainage zones. As tectonic plates move about the Earth they can rise and fall due to changing pressures and the presence of glaciers. If a beach is moving upwards relative to other plates this is known as isostatic change and raised beaches can be formed.

5.2.4. Coastal Landforms

5.2.4.1. Spits

If the coast suddenly changes direction, especially around an estuary, spits are likely to form. LSD pushes sediment along the beach but when it reaches a turn as in the diagram, the LSD does not always easily turn with it, especially near an estuary where the outward flow from a river may push sediment away from the coast. The area may be also be shielded from wave action, preventing much LSD. On the side of the headland receiving weaker waves, shingle and other large sediments will build up under the water where waves are not strong enough to move them along. This provides a good place for smaller sediments to build up to sea level. The sediment, after passing the headland will accumulate on the other side and not continue down the beach, sheltered both by the headland and the shingle.

Slowly over time sediment simply builds on this area, extending the spit outwards, forming a barrier of sand. Once in a while, the wind direction will change and come from the other direction. During this period the sediment will be pushed along in the other direction. The spit will start to grow backwards, forming a 'hook'. After this time the spit will grow again in the original direction. Eventually the spit will not be able to grow any further because it is no longer sufficiently sheltered from erosion by waves, or because the estuary current prevents sediment resting. Usually in the salty but calm waters behind the spit there will form a salt marshland. Spits often form around the breakwater of artificial harbours requiring dredging.

Occasionally, if there is no estuary then it is possible for the spit to grow across to the other side of the bay and form what is called a bar, or barrier. Barriers come in several varieties, but all form in a manner similar to spits. They usually enclose a bay to form a lagoon. They can join two headlands or join a headland to the mainland. When an island is joined to the mainland with a bar or barrier it is known as a tombolo. This usually occurs due to wave refraction, but can also be caused by isostatic change, a change in the level of the land.

5.3. Landscape Ecology and Environment

Landscape ecology is a sub-discipline of ecology and geography that address how spatial variation in the landscape affects ecological processes such as the distribution and flow of energy, materials and individuals in the environment. Landscape ecology typically deals with problems in an applied and holistic context.

5.3.1. Terminology

The term landscape ecology was coined by Carl Troll, a German geographer in 1939. He developed this terminology and many early concepts of landscape ecology as part of his early work applying aerial photograph interpretation to studies of interactions between environment and vegetation.

Heterogeneity is the measure of how different parts of a landscape are from one another. Landscape ecology looks at how spatial structure affects organism abundance at the landscape level, as well as the behaviour and functioning of the landscape as a whole. This includes the study of the pattern, or the internal order of a landscape, on process, or the continuous operation of functions of organisms. Landscape ecology also includes geomorphology as applied to the design and architecture of landscapes. Geomorphology is the study of how geological formations are responsible for the structure of a landscape.

5.3.2. Evolution of Theory

One central landscape ecology theory originated from MacArthur

& Wilson's *The Theory of Island Biogeography*. This work considered the assembly of flora and fauna on islands as the result of colonisation from a mainland stock and stochastic extinction. The concepts of island biogeography were generalised from physical islands to abstract patches of habitat by Levins' metapopulation model. This generalisation spurred the growth of landscape ecology by providing conservation biologists a new tool to assess how habitat fragmentation affects population viability. Recent growth of landscape ecology owes much to the development of geographic information systems (GIS) technology and the availability of large-extent habitat data.

Landscape ecology developed in Europe from historical planning on human-dominated landscapes. In North America, concepts from general ecology theory were integrated. While general ecology theory and its sub-disciplines focused on the study of more homogenous, discrete community units organised in a hierarchical structure, landscape ecology built upon heterogeneity in space and time, and frequently included human-caused landscape changes in theory and application of concepts.

By 1980, landscape ecology was a discrete, established discipline, marked by the organisation of the International Association for Landscape Ecology (IALE) in 1982 and landmark book publications defining the scope and goals of the discipline, including Naveh and Lieberman and Forman and Godron. Forman wrote that although study of "the ecology of spatial configuration at the human scale" was barely a decade old, there was strong potential for theory development and application of the conceptual framework. Today, theory and application of landscape ecology continues to develop through a need for innovative applications in a changing landscape and environment. Landscape ecology today relies more on advanced technologies such as remote sensing, GIS, and simulation models, with associated development of powerful quantitative methods to examine the interactions of patterns and processes.

5.3.3. Important of Landscape Ecology

Landscape ecology not only embraced a new vocabulary of terms but also incorporated general ecology theory terms in new ways. Many of the terms used in landscape ecology are as interconnected and interrelated as the discipline itself. Landscape can be defined as an area containing two or more ecosystems in close proximity.

5.3.3.1. Scale and heterogeneity

A main concept in landscape ecology is scale. Scale represents the real world as translated onto a map, in the relationship between distance on a map image and the corresponding distance on earth. Scale is also the spatial or temporal measure of an object or a process, or level or degree of spatial resolution. Components of scale include composition, structure, and function, which are all important ecological concepts. Applied to landscape ecology, composition refers to the number of patch types represented on a landscape, and their relative abundance. For example, the amount of forest or wetland, the length of forest edge, or the density of roads can be aspects of landscape composition. Structure is determined by the composition, the configuration, and the proportion of different patches across the landscape, while function refers to how each element in the landscape interacts based on its life cycle events. Pattern is the term for the contents and internal order of a heterogeneous area of land. A landscape with structure and pattern implies that it has spatial heterogeneity, or the uneven, non-random distribution of objects across the landscape. Heterogeneity is a key element of landscape ecology that separates this discipline from other branches of ecology.

5.3.3.2. Patch and mosaic

Patch, a term fundamental to landscape ecology, is defined as a relatively homogeneous area that differs from its surroundings. Patches are the basic unit of the landscape that change and fluctuate, a process called patch dynamics. Patches have a definite shape and spatial configuration, and can be described compositionally by internal variables such as number of trees, number of tree species, height of trees, or other similar measurements.

5.3.3.3. Boundary and edge

Landscape patches have a boundary between them which can be

defined or fuzzy. The zone composed of the edges of adjacent ecosystems is the boundary. Edge means the portion of an ecosystem near its perimeter, where influences of the adjacent patches can cause an environmental difference between the interior of the patch and its edge. This edge effect includes a distinctive species composition or abundance in the outer part of the landscape patch. For example, when a landscape is a mosaic of perceptibly different types, such as a forest adjacent to a grassland, the edge is the location where the two types adjoin. In a continuous landscape, such as a forest giving way to open woodland, the exact edge location is fuzzy and is sometimes determined by a local gradient exceeding a threshold, such as the point where the tree cover falls below thirty-five percent.

5.3.3.4. Ecotones, ecoclines, and ecotopes

A type of boundary is the ecotone, or the transitional zone between two communities. Ecotones can arise naturally, such as a lakeshore, or can be human-created, such as a cleared agricultural field from a forest. The ecotonal community retains characteristics of each bordering community and often contains species not found in the adjacent communities. Classic examples of ecotones include fencerows; forest to marshlands transitions; forest to grassland transitions; or land-water interfaces such as riparian zones in forests. Characteristics of ecotones include vegetational sharpness, physiognomic change, occurrence of a spatial community mosaic, many exotic species, ecotonal species, spatial mass effect, and species richness higher or lower than either side of the ecotone.

An ecocline is another type of landscape boundary, but it is a gradual and continuous change in environmental conditions of an ecosystem or community. Ecoclines help explain the distribution and diversity of organisms within a landscape because certain organisms survive better under certain conditions, which change along the ecocline. They contain heterogeneous communities which are considered more environmentally stable than those of ecotones.

An ecotope is a spatial term representing the smallest ecologically-distinct unit in mapping and classification of landscapes. Relatively homogeneous, they are spatially-explicit landscape units used to stratify landscapes into ecologically distinct features for measurement and mapping of landscape structure, function, and change over time, and to examine the effects of disturbance and fragmentation.

5.3.3.5. *Disturbance and fragmentation*

Disturbance is an event that significantly alters the pattern of variation in the structure or function of a system, while fragmentation is the breaking up of a habitat, ecosystem, or land-use type into smaller parcels. Disturbance is generally considered a natural process. Fragmentation causes land transformation, an important current process in landscapes as more and more development occurs.

5.3.4. Landscape Ecology Theory

5.3.4.1. *Elements of landscape ecology theory*

Landscape ecology, as a theory, stresses the role of human impacts on landscape structures and functions and proposes ways for restoring degraded landscapes. Landscape ecology explicitly includes humans as entities that cause functional changes on the landscape. Landscape ecology theory includes the landscape stability principle, which emphasises the importance of landscape structural heterogeneity in developing resistance to disturbances, recovery from disturbances, and promoting total system stability. This principle is a major contribution to general ecological theories which highlight the importance of relationships among the various components of the landscape. Integrity of landscape components helps maintain resistance to external threats, including development and land transformation by human activity. Analysis of land use changes has included a strongly geographical approach within landscape ecology. This has led to acceptance of the idea of multifunctional properties of landscapes. There are still calls for a more unified theory of landscape ecology due to differences in professional opinion among landscape ecologists, and the interdisciplinary approach to the discipline.

5.3.4.2. *Landscape ecology application*

Research directions

Developments in landscape ecology illustrate the important

relationships between spatial patterns and ecological processes, and incorporate quantitative methods that link spatial patterns and ecological processes at broad spatial and temporal scales. This linkage of time, space, and environmental change can assist land managers in applying land management plans to solve environmental problems. The increased attention in recent years on spatial dynamics has highlighted the need for new quantitative methods that can analyse patterns, determine the importance of spatially explicit processes on the landscape, and develop reliable landscape models. Multivariate analysis techniques, a type of statistics incorporating many variables, are frequently used to examine landscape level vegetation patterns. A number of studies in riparian systems and wetlands use a variety of statistical techniques, such as cluster analysis, canonical correspondence analysis (CCA), or detrended correspondence analysis (DCA), for classifying vegetation. Gradient analysis is another way to determine the vegetation structure across a landscape, or to help delineate critical wetland habitat for conservation or mitigation purposes.

Climate change is another major component in structuring current research in landscape ecology. Ecotones, as a basic unit in landscape studies, may have significance for management under climate change scenarios, since change effects are likely to be seen at ecotones first because of the unstable nature of a fringe habitat. Research in northern regions has examined landscape ecological processes, such as the accumulation of snow during winter, snow melting, freeze-thaw action, percolation, soil moisture variation, and temperature regimes through long-term measurements in Norway. The study analyses gradients across space and time between ecosystems of the central high mountains to determine relationships between distribution patterns of animals in their environment. Looking at where animals live, and how vegetation shifts over time, may provide insight into changes in snow and ice over long periods of time across the landscape as a whole.

Other landscape-scale studies maintain that human impact is likely the main determinant of landscape pattern over much of the globe. Landscapes may become substitutes for biodiversity measures because plant and animal composition differs between samples taken from sites within different landscape categories. Taxa, or different species, can "leak" from one habitat into another, which has implications for landscape ecology. As human land use practices expand, and continue to increase the proportion of edges in landscapes, the effects of this leakage across edges on assemblage integrity may become more significant and important in conservation because taxa may be conserved across landscape levels, if not at local levels.

5.3.4.3. Relationship to other disciplines

Landscape ecology has important links to application-oriented disciplines such as agriculture and forestry. In agriculture, landscape ecology has introduced new options for the control and management of environmental threats brought about by the intensification of agricultural practices. Agriculture has always been a strong human impact on ecosystems. In forestry, changes in consumer needs have changed conservation and use of forested landscapes from structuring stands for fuelwood and timber to ordering stands across landscapes to enhance aesthetics, habitats and biological diversity. Landscape forestry provides methods, concepts, and analytic procedures for shifting management from traditional to landscape forestry. Landscape ecology has been cited as a major contributor to the development of fisheries biology as a distinct biological science discipline, and is frequently incorporated in study design for wetland delineation in hydrology.

Geomatics is the filed of gathering, storing, processing, and delivering of geographic information, or spatially referenced information. Geomatrics includes geodesy and G.I.S. and remote sensing (the short or large-scale acquisition of information of an object or phenomenon, by the use of either recording or real-time sensing device(s) that is not in physical or intimate contact with the object).

Environmental geography is a branch of geography that describes the spatial aspects of interactions between humans and the natural world. The branch bridges the divide between human and physical geography and thus requires an understanding of the dynamics of geology, meteorology, hydrology, biogeography, and geomorphology, as well as the ways in which human societies conceptualise the environment. Although the branch was previously more visible in research than at present with theories such as environmental determinism linking society with the environment. It has largely become the domain of the study of environmental management or anthropogenic influences on the environment and vice a versa.

5.4. Conclusion

Landforms evolve in response to a combination of natural and anthropogenic processes. The landscape is built up through tectonic uplift and volcanism. Denudation occurs by erosion and mass wasting, which produces sediment that is transported and deposited elsewhere within the landscape or off the coast. Landscapes are also lowered by subsidence, either due to tectonics or physical changes in underlying sedimentary deposits. These processes are each influenced differently by climate, ecology, and human activity.

Practical applications of geomorphology include measuring the effects of climate change, hazard assessments including landslide prediction and mitigation, river control and restoration, coastal protection, and assessing the presence of water on Mars. Paleogeomorphology is the study of the geomorphology of all or part of the earth's surface at some time in the earth's past.

References

Alan R.H. Baker and Mark Billinge (eds.), *Period and Place: Research Methods in Historical Geography*, 1982.

____________ and Derek Gregory (eds.), *Explorations in Historical Geography*, 1984.

Dodgshon, R.A. and R.A. Butlin, ed., *An Historical Geography of England and Wales*, second edition, London, 1990.

Gary A. Goreham, *Encyclopedia of rural America: the land and people*, (editor) Santa Barbara, Calif.: ABC-CLIO, 1997.

Hayes-Bohanan, James, *What is Environmental Geography, Anyway?*. Retrieved on October 9, 2006.

Holdsworth D.W., "Historical geography: New ways of imaging and seeing the past", *Progress in Human Geography*, 2003.

____________ ., "Historical geography: The ancients and the

moderns – generational vitality", *Progress in Human Geography*, 2002.

Knowles A.K., *Historical Geography*, vol. 33, 2005.

McManis, Douglas R., *Historical geography of the United States; a bibliography, excluding Alaska and Hawaii*, Eastern Michigan University, 1965.

Mittal, P. & Dua, Geeta, *Historical Geography of India*, 2 Vols., 2005

Smith, C.T., *An Historical Geography of Western Europe Before 1800*, 1967.

Sullivan, Dan, *Mapmaking and its History*, Rutgers University, 2000.

Ward, Dederick C., Wheeler, Marjorie W. and Bier, Robert A., Jr., *Geologic reference sources: a subject and regional bibliography of publications and maps in the geological sciences*, 2nd ed. Metuchen, NJ: Scarecrow Press, 1981.

William Norton, *Historical Analysis in Geography*, 1984.

6

Political Geography

6.1. Introduction

The origins of political geography lie in the origins of human geography itself and the early practitioners were concerned mainly with the military and political consequences of the relationships between physical geography, state territories, and state power. In particular there was a close association with regional geography, with its focus on the unique characteristics of regions, and environmental determinism with its emphasis on the influence of the physical environment on human activities.

The German geographer Friedrich Ratzel, in 1897 in his book *Politische Geographie,* developed the concept of Lebensraum (living space) which explicitly linked the cultural growth of a nation with territorial expansion, and which was later used to provide academic legitimation for the imperialist expansion of the German Third Reich in the 1930s.

The British geographer Halford Mackinder was also heavily influenced by environmental determinism and in developing his concept of the 'geopolitical pivot of history' or heartland (first developed in 1904) he argued that the era of sea power was coming to an end and that land based powers were in the ascendant, and, in particular, that whoever controlled the heartland of 'Euro-Asia' would control the world. This theory involved concepts diametrically opposed to the ideas of Alfred Thayer Mahan about the significance of sea power in world conflict. The heartland theory hypothesised the possibility of a huge empire being created which didn't need to use coastal or transoceanic transport to supply its military industrial complex, and that this empire could not be defeated by the rest of the world coalitioned against it. This perspective proved influential throughout the period of the Cold War, underpinning military thinking about the creation of buffer states between East and West in central Europe.

The heartland theory depicted a world divided into a Heartland (Eastern Europe/Western Russia); World Island (Eurasia and Africa); Peripheral Islands (British Isles, Japan, Indonesia and Australia) and New World (The Americas). Mackinder claimed that whoever controlled the Heartland would have control of the world. He used this warning to politically influence events such as the Treaty of Versailles, where buffer states were created between the USSR and Germany, to prevent either of the them controlling the Heartland. At the same time, Ratzel was creating a theory of states based around the concepts of Lebensraum and Social Darwinism. He argued that states were 'organisms' that needed sufficient room in which to live. Both of these writers created the idea of a political and geographical science, with an objective view of the world. Pre-World War II political geography was concerned largely with these issues of global power struggles and influencing state policy, and the above theories were taken on board by German geopoliticians such as Karl Haushofer who - perhaps inadvertently - greatly influenced Nazi political theory. A form of politics legitimated by 'scientific' theories such as a 'neutral' requirement for state expansion was very influential at this time.

The close association with environmental determinism and the freezing of political boundaries during the Cold War led to a considerable decline in the importance of political geography which was described by Brian Berry in 1968 as 'a moribund backwater'. Although in other areas of human geography a number of new approaches were invigorating research, including quantitative spatial science, behavioural studies, and structural marxism, these were largely ignored by political geographers whose main point of reference continued to be the regional approach. As a result much political geography of this period was descriptive with little attempt to produce generalisations from the data collected. It was not until 1976 that Richard Muir could argue that political geography might not be a dead duck but could in fact be a phoenix.

From the late-1970s onwards political geography has undergone a renaissance, and could fairly be described as one of the most dynamic of the sub-disciplines today. In part this growth has been associated with the adoption by political geographers of the approaches taken up earlier in other areas of human geography. However the recent growth in the vitality and importance of the sub-discipline is also related to changes in the world as a result of the end of the Cold War, including the emergence of a new world order, and the development of new research agendas, such as the more recent focus on social movements and political struggles going beyond the study of nationalism with its explicit territorial basis. Recently, too, there has been increasing interest in the geography of green politics, including the geopolitics of environmental protest, and in the capacity of our existing state apparatus and wider political institutions to address contemporary and future environmental problems competently.

6.2. Critical Political Geography

Critical political geography is mainly concerned with the criticism of traditional political geographies. Focusing on the expansion of geographical knowledge, within each critical argument is generally nested an alternative cause for the issue at hand, such as within Andrew Feenberg's *Critical Theory of Technology*.

Politics is the process by which groups of people make decisions. Although the term is generally applied to behaviour within civil governments, politics is observed in all human group interactions, including corporate, academic, and religious institutions. It of "social relations involving authority or power" and refers to the regulation of a political unit, and to the methods and tactics used to formulate and apply policy. Political science is the study of political behaviour and examines the acquisition and application of power.

6.2.1. Government

A government is the body that has the power to make and authority to enforce laws, rules, and policies. Governments exist in all institutions that have laws, rules, or politics.

6.2.1.1. Political power

Max Weber defined power as the ability to impose one's will

"even in the face of opposition from others," while Hannah Arendt states that "political power corresponds to the human ability not just to act but to act in concert."

Legitimate power, the power of the policeman or the referee, is the power given to an individual by a recognised authority to enforce standards of behaviour. Legitimate power is similar to coercive power in that unacceptable behaviour is punished by fine or penalty. Referent power is bestowed upon individuals by virtue of accomplishment or attitude. Fulfillment of the desire to feel similar to a celebrity or a hero is the reward for obedience. This is an example of incentive power as one rewards oneself. Expert power springs from education or experience. Following the lead of an experienced coach is often rewarded with success. Expert power is conditional to the circumstances. A brain surgeon is no help when pipes are leaking.

6.2.2. Authority and Legitimacy

Authority, in a political sense, is different from political power in that it implies legitimacy and acceptance; it implies that the person or state exercising power has a perceived right to do so. Legitimacy is an attribute of government gained through the acquisition and application of power in accordance with recognised or accepted standards or principles.

6.2.2.1. Traditional authority

Traditional authorities receive loyalty because they continue and support the preservation of existing values, the status quo. Patriarchal societies gave rise to hereditary monarchies where authority was given to descendants of previous leaders.

6.2.2.2. Charismatic authority

Charismatic authority grows out of the personal charm or the strength of an individual personality. Charismatic regimes are often short-lived, seldom outliving the charismatic figure that leads them. For a charismatic regime to survive the rule of the individual personality, it must transform its legitimacy into a different form of authority.

6.2.2.3. Legal-rational authority

Legal-rational authorities receive their ability to compel behaviour by virtue of the office that they hold. It is the authority that demands obedience to the office rather than the office holder. Modern democracies are examples of legal-rational regimes. People also abide by legal-rational authority because it makes sense to do so for their own good, as well as for the greater good of society.

6.3. SOVEREIGNTY

Sovereignty is the ability of a government to exert control over its sphere of influence free from outside interference.

6.3.1. Political Philosophies

6.3.1.1. Confucius

The Chinese philosopher Confucius was one of the first thinkers to adopt a distinct approach to political philosophy. His philosophy was "rooted in his belief that a ruler should learn self-discipline, should govern his subjects by his own example, and should treat them with love and concern." His political beliefs were strongly linked to personal ethics and morality, believing that only a morally upright ruler who possessed "de", or virtue, should be able to exercise power, and that the behaviour of an individual ought to be consistent with their rank in society. He stated that "Good government consists in the ruler being a ruler, the minister being a minister, the father being a father, and the son being a son."

6.3.1.2. Plato

The Greek philosopher Plato (428-328 BC), in his book *The Republic*, argued that all conventional political systems (democracy, monarchy, oligarchy and timarchy) were inherently corrupt, and that the state ought to be governed by an elite class of educated philosopher-rulers, who would be trained from birth and selected on the basis of aptitude. This has been characterised as authoritarian and elitist by some later scholars, notably Karl Popper in his book *The Open Society* and its Enemies, who described Plato's schemes as essentially totalitarian and criticised his apparent advocacy of censorship. The Republic has also been labelled as communist, due to its advocacy of abolishing private property and the family among the ruling classes; however, this view has been discounted by many scholars, as there are implications in the text that this will extend only to the ruling classes, and that ordinary citizens "will have enough private property to make the regulation of wealth and poverty a concern."

6.3.1.3. Aristotle

In his book *Politics*, the Greek philosopher Aristotle (384-322BC) asserted that man is, by nature, a political animal. He argued that ethics and politics are closely linked, and that a truly ethical life can only be lived by someone who participates in politics.

Like Plato, Aristotle identified a number of different forms of government, and argued that each "correct" form of government may devolve into a "deviant" form of government, in which its institutions were corrupted. According to Aristotle, kingship, with one ruler, devolves into tyranny; aristocracy, with a small group of rulers, devolves into oligarchy; and polity, with collective rule by many citizens, devolves into democracy. In this sense, Aristotle does not use the word "democracy" in its modern sense, carrying positive connotations, but in its literal sense of rule by the demos, or common people. A more accurate view of Aristotle denouncing democracy was that it was described as mob rule, or ochlocracy.

6.3.1.4. Niccolo Machiavelli

In his work *The Prince*, the Renaissance Italian political theorist Machiavelli put forward a political worldview which described practical methods for an absolute ruler to attain and maintain political power. It is from Machiavelli that the term Machiavellian is derived, referring to an amoral person who uses manipulative methods to attain power; however, many scholars have questioned this view of Machiavelli's theory, arguing that "Machiavelli did not invent 'Machiavellism' and may not even have been a 'Machiavellian' in the sense often ascribed to him." Instead, Machiavelli considered the stability of the state to be the most important goal, and argued that qualities traditionally considered morally desirable, such as generosity, were undesirable in a ruler and would lead to the loss of power. Critics of Machiavelli have often pointed out his works were studied and put into practice by leaders such as Josef Stalin, Mao Zedong, Benito Mussolini, and Adolf Hitler, who all argued their brutal programs were needed for security of the state just as Machiavelli recommended.

6.3.1.5. Thomas Hobbes

In 1651, Thomas Hobbes published his most famous work, Leviathan, in which he proposed a model of early human development to justify the creation of polities, i.e. governed bodies. Hobbes described an ideal state of nature wherein every person had equal right to every resource in nature and was free to use any means to acquire those resources. He claimed that such an arrangement created a "war of all against all." Hobbes' view can therefore be interpreted as a defense of absolutism, arguing that human beings enter into a social contract for their protection and agree to obey the dictates of the sovereign; in Hobbes' worldview, "the sovereign is nothing more than the personal embodiment of orderly government."

6.3.1.6. John Locke

The English philosopher John Locke was "one of the greatest philosophers in Europe at the end of the seventeenth century". His political philosophy is contained primarily in his Two Treatises of Government. In the First Treatise of Government, Locke refutes the theory of the Divine Right of Kings as put forward by Robert Filmer; he "minutely examines key Biblical passages" and concludes that absolute monarchy is not supported by Christian theology. "Locke singles out Filmer's contention that men are not 'naturally free' as the key issue, for that is the 'ground'...on which Filmer erects his argument for the claim that all 'legitimate' government is 'absolute monarchy'."

6.3.1.7. Jean-Jacques Rousseau

The 18th century French philosopher Jean-Jacques Rousseau, in his book The Social Contract, put forward a system of political thought which was closely related to those of Hobbes and Locke, but different in important respects. Rousseau argues that the people may need a "lawgiver" to draw up a constitution and system of laws, because the general will, "while always morally sound, is sometimes mistaken".

Rousseau's thought has been seen by some scholars as contradictory and inconsistent, and as not addressing the fundamental contradiction between individual freedom and subordination to the needs of society, "the tension that seems to exist between liberalism and communitarianism". The Catholic Encyclopedia further argues that Rousseau's concept of the general will would inevitably lead to "the suppression of personality, the reign of force and caprice, the tyranny of the multitude, the despotism of the crowd", i.e. the subordination of the individual to society as a whole.

6.3.1.8. John Stuart Mill

In the 19th century, John Stuart Mill pioneered the liberal conception of politics. He saw democracy as the major political development of his era and, in his book *On Liberty*, advocated stronger protection for individual rights against government and the rule of the majority. He argued that liberty was the most important right of human beings, and that the only just cause for interfering with the liberty of another person was self-protection. One commentator refers to *On Liberty* as "the strongest and most eloquent defense of liberalism that we have." Mill also emphasised the importance of freedom of speech, claiming that "we can never be sure that the opinion we are attempting to stifle is a false opinion, and if we were sure, stifling it would be an evil still."

6.3.1.9. Karl Marx

Karl Marx was among the most influential political philosophers of history. His theories, collectively termed Marxism, were critical of capitalism and argued that in the due course of history, there would be an "inevitable breakdown of capitalism for economic reasons, to be replaced by communism." He defined history in terms of the class struggle between the bourgeoisie, or property-owning classes, and the proletariat, or workers, a struggle intensified by industrialisation: "The development of Modern

Industry, therefore, cuts from under its feet the very foundation on which the bourgeoisie produces and appropriates products. What the bourgeoisie therefore produces, above all, are its own grave-diggers. Its fall and the victory of the proletariat are equally inevitable. Utopia for Marx was the classless society in which the state and the church would be very weak or nonexistent. The workers ultimately would own the means of production, state ownership would be a mere transition period, therefore the people would be free. Because the state as Marx knew it would practically disappear over time, there would be no need for borders so individuals would be free to move from nation to nation without prosecution. This latter idea of internationalism is the direct opposition to the Nazi utopia of the pure race and national socialism. This can not be said of capitalism which have no definite instance on the free moviment of labor and capital across national boundaries. Although Marxism is mostly associated with the Soviet Union for obvious reasons, one may also see in the European Union many but not all of Marx's ideas such as universal health care, open border and the free moviment of people, and lower levels of economic inequality.

The multiple notions of political power that are put forth range from conventional views that simply revolve around the actions of politicians to those who view political power as an insidious form of institutionalised social control - most notably "anarchists" and "radical capitalists". The main views of political power revolve around normative, post-modern, and pragmatic perspectives.

6.3.2. Faces of Power Debate

The faces of power debate has coalesced into a viable conception of three dimensions of power including decision-making, agenda-setting, and preference-shaping. The decision-making dimension was first put forth by Robert Dahl, who advocated the notion that political power is based in the formal political arena and is measured through voting patterns and the decisions made by politicians. This view has been criticised by many as simplistic, notably by the sociologist G. William Domhoff, who argues that political and economic power is monopolised by the "elite classes".

A second dimension to the notion of political power was added by academics Peter Bachrach and Morton Baratz involving "agenda-setting". Bachrach and Baratz viewed power as involving both the formal political arena and behind the scenes agenda-setting by elite groups who could be either politicians and/or others, often with a hidden agenda that most of the public may not be aware of. The third dimension of power was added by British academic Steven Lukes who felt that even with this second dimension, some other traits of political power needed to be addressed through the concept of 'preference-shaping'.

This third dimension is inspired by many Neo-Gramscian views such as cultural hegemony and deals with how civil society and the general public have their preferences shaped for them by those in power through the use of propaganda or the media. Ultimately, this third dimension holds that the general public may not be aware of what decisions are actually in their interest due to the invisible power of elites who work to distort their perceptions. Critics of this view claim that such notions are themselves elitist, which Lukes then clearly admits as one problem of this view and yet clarifies that as long as those who make claims that preferences are being shaped explain their own interests etc., there is room for more transparency.

6.4. Political Spectra

6.4.1. Left-Right Politics

Most political analysts and politicians divide politics into left wing and right wing politics, often also using the idea of center politics as a middle path of policy between the right and left. This classification is comparatively recent, and dates from the French Revolution era, when those members of the National Assembly who opposed the monarchy sat on the left, while those who supported it sat on the right.

The meaning of left-wing and right-wing varies considerably between different countries and at different times, but broadly speaking, it can be said that the right wing is often linked to moral and social conservatism, law and order, and religion, while the left wing is often linked with redistribution of wealth and resources towards the poorer or less successful sections of society (which are generally perceived by the left as unfairly disadvantaged), and with secularism. The right wing is more often linked to the idea of social equity, and the left wing to the idea of social equality. According to Norberto Bobbio, one of the major exponents of this distinction, the Left believes in attempting to eradicate social inequality, while the Right regards most social inequality as the result of ineradicable natural inequalities, and sees attempts to enforce social equality as utopian or authoritarian.

Some ideologies, notably Christian Democracy, claim to combine left and right wing politics; according to Geoffrey K. Roberts and Patricia Hogwood, "In terms of ideology, Christian Democracy has incorporated many of the views held by liberals, conservatives and socialists within a wider framework of moral and Christian principles." Movements which claim or formerly claimed to be above the left-right divide include Gaullism in France, Peronism in Argentina, and National Action Politics in Mexico.

6.4.1.1. Authoritarian-libertarian

While left and right refer to different methods of developing an economically stable and just society, authoritarianism and libertarianism refer to the amount of individual freedom each person possesses in that society relative to the state. One author describes authoritarian political systems as those where "individual rights and goals are subjugated to group goals, expectations and conformities", while a libertarian political system is one in which individual rights and civil liberties are paramount. More extreme than libertarians are anarchists, who argue for the total abolition of government, while the most extreme authoritarians are totalitarians who support state control over all aspects of society.

Authoritarianism and libertarianism are separate concepts from the left-right political axis. For instance, classical liberalism and contemporary American libertarianism are socially liberal, but reject extensive governmental intervention in the economy and welfare. According to the libertarian Institute for Humane Studies, "the libertarian, or 'classical liberal,' perspective is that individual well-being, prosperity, and social harmony are fostered by 'as much liberty as possible' and 'as little government as necessary." These three forms of authority are said to appear in a "hierarchical development order"; states progress from charismatic authority, to traditional authority, and finally reach the state of rational-legal authority which is characteristic of a modern liberal democracy.

6.5. International Relations

International relations (IR), a branch of political science, is the study of foreign affairs and global issues among states within the international system, including the roles of states, inter-governmental organisations (IGOs), non-governmental organisations (NGOs), and multinational corporations (MNCs). It is both an academic and public policy field, and can be either positive or normative as it both seeks to analyse as well as formulate the foreign policy of particular states.

Apart from political science, IR draws upon such diverse fields as economics, history, law, philosophy, geography, sociology, anthropology, psychology, and cultural studies. It involves a diverse range of issues, from globalisation and its impacts on societies and state sovereignty to ecological sustainability, nuclear proliferation, nationalism, economic development, terrorism, organised crime, human security, and human rights.

The history of international relations is often traced back to the Peace of Westphalia of 1648, where the modern state system was developed. Prior to this, the European medieval organisation of political authority was based on a vaguely hierarchical religious order. Westphalia instituted the legal concept of sovereignty, which essentially meant that rulers, or the legitimate sovereigns, would recognise no internal equals within a defined territory and no external superiors as the ultimate authority within the territory's sovereign borders. Classical Greek and Roman authority at times resembled the Westphalian system, but both lacked the notion of sovereignty.

Westphalia encouraged the rise of independent nation-state, the institutionalisation of diplomacy and armies. This particular European system was exported to the Americas, Africa, and Asia via colonialism and the "standards of civilisation". The contemporary international system was finally established through decolonisation during the Cold War. However, this is somewhat over-simplified. While the nation-state system is considered "modern", many states have not incorporated the system and are termed "pre-modern". Further, a handful of states have moved beyond the nation-state system and can be considered "post-modern". The ability of contemporary IR discourse to explain the relations of these different types of states is disputed. "Levels of analysis" is a way of looking at the international system, which includes the individual level, the domestic nation-state as a unit, the international level of transnational and intergovernmental affairs, and the global level.

Initially, international relations as a distinct field of study was almost entirely British-centred. In 1919, the Chair in International Politics established at the University of Wales, Aberystwyth, from an endowment given by David Davies, became the first academic position dedicated to IR. In the early 1920s, the London School of Economics' department of International Relations was founded at the behest of Nobel Peace Prize winner Phillip Noel-Baker. In 1927 the first university institution entirely dedicated to the study of IR, the Graduate Institute of International Studies, was founded in Geneva, Switzerland; it sought to supply a pool of specialised personnel for the League of Nations.

6.5.1. IR Theories

IR theories can be roughly divided into one of two epistemological camps: "positivist" and "post-positivist". Positivist theories aim to replicate the methods of the natural sciences by analysing the impact of material forces. They typically focus on features of international relations such as state interactions, size of military forces, balance of powers etc. Post-positivist epistemology rejects the idea that the social world can be studied in an objective and value-free way. It rejects the central ideas of neo-realism/ liberalism, such as rational choice theory, on the grounds that the scientific method cannot be applied to the social world and that a 'science' of IR is impossible. A key difference between the two positions is that while positivist theories, such as neo-realism, offer causal explanations post-positivist theories focus instead on constitutive questions, for instance what is meant by 'power';

what makes it up, how it is experienced and how it is reproduced. Often, post-positivist theories explicitly promote a normative approach to IR, by considering ethics. This is something which has often been ignored under 'traditional' IR as positivist theories make a distinction between 'facts' and normative judgments, or 'values'.

6.5.2. Positivist Theories

6.5.2.1. Liberalism/Idealism/Liberal Internationalism

Liberal international relations theory arose after World War I in response to the inability of states to control and limit war in their international relations. Early adherents include Woodrow Wilson and Norman Angell, who argued variously that states mutually gained from cooperation and that war was so destructive to be essentially futile. Liberalism was not recognised as a coherent theory as such until it was collectively and derisively termed idealism by E. H. Carr. A new version of "idealism," centered around human rights as basis of the legitimacy of international law, was advanced by Hans Köchler.

6.5.2.2. Realism

Realism was a response to liberalism that chiefly denies that states seek to cooperate. Early realists such as E.H. Carr, Daniel Bernhard and Hans Morgenthau argued that, for the purpose of increasing their security, states are self-interested, power-seeking rational actors. Any cooperation between states is explained as purely incidental. Realists saw World War II as the vindication of their theory. It should be noted that classical writers such as Thucydides, Machiavelli, and Hobbes are often cited as the "founding fathers" of realism by contemporary self-described realists. However, while their work may support realist doctrine, it is not likely that they would have classified themselves as realists.

6.5.2.3. Neorealism

Neorealism is largely the work of Kenneth Waltz. While retaining the empirical observations of realism, that international relations are characterised by antagonistic interstate relations, neorealists point to the anarchic structure of the international system as the cause. They reject explanations that take account of states' domestic characteristics. States are compelled by relative gains and balance against concentration of power. Unlike realism, neo-realism seeks to be scientific and more positivist.What also distinguishes neo-realism from realism is that the former does not accept the latter's emphasis on the behavioural explanation of international relations.

6.5.2.4. Neoliberalism

Neoliberalism seeks to update liberalism by accepting the neorealist presumption that states are the key actors in international relations, but still maintains that non-state actors (NSAs) and intergovernmental organisations (IGOs) matter. Proponents such as Maria Chattha argue that states will cooperate irrespective of relative gains, and are thus concerned with absolute gains. The growing interdependence throughout the Cold War through international institutions means that neo-liberalism is also called liberal institutionalism. This also means that nations are, in essence, free to make their own choices as to how they will go about conducting policy without any international organisations blocking a nation's right to sovereignty. Neoliberalism also contains an economic theory that is based on the use of open and free markets with little, if any, government intervention to prevent monopolies and other conglomerates from forming.

6.5.3. Post-positivist/Reflectivist Theories

6.5.3.1. International society theory

International society theory, also called the English School, focuses on the shared norms and values of states and how they regulate international relations. Examples of such norms include diplomacy, order, and international law. Unlike neo-realism, it is not necessarily positivist. Theorists have focused particularly on humanitarian intervention, and are subdivided between solidarists, who tend to advocate it more, and pluralists, who place greater value in order and sovereignty. Nicholas Wheeler is a prominent solidarist, while Hedley Bull and Robert H. Jackson are perhaps the best known pluralist.

6.5.3.2. Social constructivism

Social constructivism encompasses a broad range of theories that aim to address questions of ontology, such as the Structure and agency debate, as well as questions of epistemology, such as the "material/ideational" debate that concerns the relative role of material forces versus ideas. Constructivism is not a theory of IR, for example in the manner of neo-realism, but instead is a social theory.

Constructivism in IR can be divided into what Hopf calls 'conventional' and 'critical' constructivism. Common to all varieties of constructivism is an interest in the role that ideational forces play. The most famous constructivist scholar, Alexander Wendt noted in a 1992 article in International Organisation, that "anarchy is what states make of it". By this he means that the anarchical structure that neo-realists claim governs state interaction is in fact a phenomenon that is socially constructed and reproduced by states. Critics, however, abound from both sides of the epistemological divide: Post-positivists say the focus on the state at the expense of ethnicity/race/class/gender makes social constructivism yet another positivist theory. The use of implicit rational choice theory by Wendt has also raised criticisms from scholars such as Steven Smith. Positivist scholars of liberalism/realism hold that the theory forgoes too many positivist assumptions for it to be considered positivist.

6.5.4. Critical Theory

Critical international relations theory is the application of 'critical theory' to international relations. Proponents such as Andrew Linklater, Robert W. Cox and Ken Booth focus on the need for human emancipation from States. Hence, it is "critical" of mainstream IR theories that tend to be state-centric.

6.5.4.1. Marxism

Marxist and Neo-Marxist theories of IR reject the realist/liberal view of state conflict or cooperation; instead focusing on the economic and material aspects. It makes the assumption that the economy trumps other concerns; allowing for the elevation of class as the focus of study. Marxists view the international system as an integrated capitalist system in pursuit of capital accumulation. Thus, the period of colonialism brought in sources for raw materials and captive markets for exports, while decolonialisation brought new opportunities in the form of dependence.

Linked in with Marxist theories is dependency theory which argues that developed countries, in their pursuit of power, penetrate developing states through political advisors, missionaries, experts and MNCs to integrate them into the integrated capitalist system in order to appropriate natural resources and foster dependence by developing countries on developed countries.

Marxist theories receive scant attention in the United States where no significant socialist party ever existed. It is more common in parts of Europe and is one of the most important theoretic contributions of Latin American academia, for example through Liberation theology.

6.5.5. Poststructuralist Theories

Poststructuralist theories of IR developed in the 1980s from postmodernist studies in political science. Post-structuralism explores the deconstruction of concepts traditionally not problematic in IR, such as 'power' and 'agency' and examines how the construction of these concepts shapes international relations. The examination of 'narratives' plays an important part in poststructuralist analysis, for example feminist poststructuralist work has examined the role that 'women' play in global society and how they are constructed in war as 'innocent' and 'civilians'.

6.6. Concepts in International Relations

6.6.1. Systemic Level Concepts

International relations is often viewed in terms of levels of analysis, the systemic level concepts are those broad concepts that define and shape an international milieu, characterised by Anarchy.

6.6.2. Power

The concept of Power in international relations can be described as the degree of resources, capabilities, and influence in international affairs. It is often divided up into the concepts of hard power and soft power, hard power relating primarily to coercive power, such as the use of force, and soft power commonly covering economics, diplomacy and cultural influence. However, there is no clear dividing line between the two forms of power.

6.6.3. Polarity

Polarity in International Relations refers to the arrangement of power within the international system. The concept arose from bipolarity during the Cold War, with the international system dominated by the conflict between two superpowers, and has been applied retrospectively. Consequently, the international system prior to 1945 can be described as multi-polar, with power being shared among Great powers. The collapse of the Soviet Union in 1991 has led to what some would call unipolarity, with the United States as a sole superpower. Several theories of international relations draw upon the idea of polarity.

The balance of power was a concept prevalent in Europe prior to the First World War, the thought being that by balancing power blocs it would create stability and prevent war. Theories of the balance of power gained prominence again during the Cold War, being a central mechanism of Kenneth Waltz's Neorealism. Here, the concepts of balancing (rising in power to counter another) and bandwagonning are developed.

Hegemonic stability theory also draws upon the idea of Polarity, specifically the state of unipolarity. Hegemony is the preponderance of power at one pole in the international system, and the theory argues this is stable configuration because of mutual gains by both the dominant power and others in the international system. This is contrary to many Neorealist arguments, particularly made by Kenneth Waltz, stating that the end of the Cold War and the state of unipolarity is an unstable configuration that will inevitably change.

This can be expressed in Power transition theory, which states that it is likely that a great power would challenge a hegemon after a certain period, resulting in a major war. It suggests that while hegemony can control the occurrence of wars, it also results in the creation of one. Its main proponent, A.F.K. Organski, argued this based on the occurrence of previous wars during British, Portuguese and Dutch hegemony.

6.6.4. Interdependence

Many advocate that the current international system is characterised by growing interdependence; the mutual responsibility and dependency on others. Advocates of this point to growing globalisation, particularly with international economic interaction. The role of international institutions, and widespread acceptance of a number of operating principles in the international system, reinforces ideas that relations are characterised by interdependence.

6.6.5. Dependency

Dependency theory is a theory most commonly associated with Marxism, stating that a set of Core states exploit a set of weaker Periphery states for their prosperity. Various versions of the theory suggest that this is either an inevitability (standard dependency theory), or use the theory to highlight the necessity for change (Neo-Marxist).

6.6.6. Unit-level Concepts in International Relations

As a level of analysis the unit level is often referred to as the state level, as it locates its explanation at the level of the state, rather than the international system.

6.6.6.1. Regime type

It is often considered that a states regime type can dictate the way that a state interacts with others in the international system. Democratic Peace Theory is a theory that suggests that the nature of democracy means that democratic countries will not go to war with each other. The justifications for this are that democracies externalise their norms and only go to war for just causes, and that democracy encourages mutual trust and respect. Communism justifies a world revolution, which similarly would lead to peaceful coexistence, based on a proletarian global society.

6.6.6.2. Revisionism/Status quo

States can be classified by whether they accept the international status quo, or are revisionist, i.e. want change. Revisionist states seek to fundamentally change the rules and practices of international relations, feeling disadvantaged by the status quo. They see the international system as a largely western creation which serves to reinforce current realities. Japan is an example of a state that has gone from being a revisionist state to one that is satisfied with the status quo, because the status quo is now beneficial to it.

6.6.6.3. Religion

It is often considered that religion can have an effect on the way a state acts within the international system. Religion is visible as an organising principle particularly for Islamic states, whereas secularism sits at the other end of the spectrum, with the separation of state and religion being responsible for the Liberal tradition.

6.6.6.4. Individual or sub-unit level concepts

The level beneath the unit (state) level can be useful both for explaining factors in International Relations that other theories fail to explain, and for moving away from a state-centric view of international relations.

Psychological factors in International Relations - Evaluating psychological factors in international relations comes from the understanding that a state is not a 'black box' as proposed by Realism, and that there may be other influences on foreign policy decisions. Examining the role of personalities in the decision making process can have some explanatory power, as can the role of misperception between various actors. A prominent application of sub-unit level psychological factors in international relations is the concept of Groupthink, another is the propensity of policymakers to think in terms of analogies.

Bureaucratic politics - Looks at the role of the bureaucracy in decision making, and sees decisions as a result of bureaucratic in-fighting, and as having been shaped by various constraints. Religious, Ethnic, and secessionist groups - Viewing these aspects of the sub-unit level has explanatory power with regards to ethnic conflicts, religious wars, transnational diaspora and other actors which do not consider themselves to fit with the defined state boundaries. This is particularly useful in the context of the pre-modern world of weak states.

6.6.7. Institutions in International Relations

International institutions form a vital part of contemporary International Relations. Much interaction at the system level is governed by them, and they outlaw some traditional institutions and practices of International Relations, such as the use of war.

This principle guides the formation of institutions based on three characteristics: irreducibility, where some issues must be adjudicated at the global level; subsidiarity, which limits the scope of global authority to truly global issues while smaller-scope issues are regulated at lower levels; and heterogeneity, which allows for diverse forms of local and regional institutions as long as they meet global obligations.

6.7. Geopolitics

Geopolitics is the study that analyses geography, history and social science with reference to spatial politics and patterns at various scales (ranging from home, city, region, state to international and cosmopolitics). It examines the political, economic and strategic significance of geography, where geography is defined in terms of the location, size, function, and relationships of places and resources.

The doctrine of Geopolitics gained attention largely through the work of Sir Halford Mackinder in England and his formulation of the Heartland Theory in 1904. The doctrine involved concepts diametrically opposed to the notion of Alfred Thayer Mahan about the significance of navies in world conflict. The Heartland theory hypothesised the possibility for a huge empire being brought into existence in the Heartland, which wouldn't need to use coastal or transoceanic transport to supply its military industrial complex but would instead use railways, and that this empire couldn't be defeated by all the rest of the world against it.

The basic notions of Mackinder's doctrine involve considering the geography of the Earth as being divided into two sections, the World Island, comprising Eurasia and Africa; and the Periphery, including the Americas, the British Isles, and Oceania. Not only was the Periphery noticeably smaller than the World Island, it necessarily required much sea transport to function at the technological level of the World Island, which contained sufficient natural resources for a developed economy. Also, the industrial centers of the Periphery were necessarily located in widely-separated locations. The World Island could send its navy to destroy each one of them in turn. It could locate its own industries in a region further inland than the Periphery could,so they would have a longer struggle reaching them, and would be facing a well-stocked industrial bastion. This region Mackinder termed the Heartland. It essentially comprised Ukraine, Western Russia, and Mitteleuropa. The Heartland contained the grain reserves of Ukraine, and many other natural resources. Mackinder's notion of geopolitics can be summed up in his saying "Who rules East Europe commands the Heartland. Who rules the Heartland commands the World-Island. Who rules the World-Island commands the world." His doctrine was influential during the World Wars and the Cold War, for Germany and later Russia each made territorial strides toward the Heartland.

Mackinder's geopolitical theory has been criticised as being too sweeping, his interpretation of human history and geography too simple and mechanistic. In his analysis of the importance of mobility, and the move from sea to rail transport, he failed to predict the revolutionary impact of air power. Critically also he underestimated the importance of social organisation in the development of power.

6.7.1. Geostrategy

Geostrategy, a subfield of geopolitics, is a type of foreign policy guided principally by geographical factors as they inform, constrain, or affect political and military planning. As with all strategies, geostrategy is concerned with matching means to ends - in this case, a country's resources with its geopolitical objectives (which can be local, regional, or global). According to Gray and Sloan, geography is "the mother of strategy."

Geostrategists, as distinct from geopoliticians, advocate proactive strategies, and approach geopolitics from a nationalist point-of-view. As with all political theories, geostrategies are relevant principally to the context in which they were devised: the nationality of the strategist, the strength of his or her country's resources, the scope of their country's goals, the political geography of the time period, and the technological factors that affect military, political, economic, and cultural engagement. Geostrategy can function normatively, advocating foreign policy based on geographic factors, analytical, describing how foreign policy is shaped by geography, or predictive, predicting a country's future foreign policy decisions on the basis of geographic factors.

Critics of geostrategy have asserted that it is a pseudoscientific gloss used by dominant nations to justify imperialist or hegemonic aspirations, or that it has been rendered irrelevant because of technological advances, or that its essentialist focus on geography leads geostrategists to incorrect conclusions about the conduct of foreign policy.

Academics, theorists, and practitioners of geopolitics have agreed upon no standard definition for "geostrategy." Most all definitions, however, emphasise the merger of strategic considerations with geopolitical factors. While geopolitics is ostensibly neutral, examining the geographic and political features of different regions, especially the impact of geography on politics, geostrategy involves comprehensive planning, assigning means for achieving national goals or securing assets of military or political significance.

As early as Herodotus, observers saw strategy as heavily influenced by the geographic setting of the actors. In History, Herodotus describes a clash of civilisations between the Egyptians, Persians, Scythians, and Greeks-all of which he believed were heavily influenced by the physical geographic setting.

Adam Heinrich Dietrich von Bülow proposed a geometrical science of strategy in the 1799 The Spirit of the Modern System of War. His system predicted that the larger states would swallow the smaller ones, resulting in eleven large states. Mackubin Thomas Owens notes the similarity between von Bülow's predictions and the map of Europe after the unification of Germany and of Italy.

Between 1890 and 1919 the world became a geostrategist's paradise, leading to the formulation of the classical geopolitical theories. The international system featured rising and falling great powers, many with global reach. There were no new frontiers for the great powers to explore or colonise-the entire world was divided between the empires and colonial powers.

The most prominent German geopolitician was General Karl Haushofer. After WWII, during the Allied occupation of Germany, the United States investigated many officials and public figures to determine if they should face charges of war crimes at the Nuremberg trials. Haushofer, an academic primarily, was interrogated by Father Edmund A. Walsh, a professor of geopolitics from the Georgetown School of Foreign Service, at the request of the U.S. authorities. Despite his involvement in crafting one of the justifications for Nazi aggression, Fr. Walsh determined that Haushofer ought not stand trial.

After the second world war, the term "geopolitics" fell into disrepute, because of its association with Nazi geopolitik. Virtually no books published between the end of WWII and the mid-1970's used the word "geopolitics" or "geostrategy" in their titles, and geopoliticians did not label themselves or their works as such.

German theories prompted a number of critical examinations of geopolitik by American geopoliticians such as Robert Strausz-Hupé, Derwent Whittlesey, and Andrew Gyorgy. As the Cold War began, N.J. Spykman and George F. Kennan laid down the foundations for the U.S. policy of containment, which would dominate Western geostrategic thought for the next forty years.

Alexander de Seversky would propose that airpower had fundamentally changed geostrategic considerations and thus proposed a "geopolitics of airpower." His ideas had some influence on the Eisenhower administration, but the ideas of Spykman and Kennan would exercise greater weight. Later during the Cold War, Colin Gray would decisively reject the idea that airpower changed geostrategic considerations, while Saul B. Cohen examined the idea of a "shatterbelt", which would eventually inform the domino theory.

6.8. Conclusion

Political geography has extended the scope of traditional political science approaches by acknowledging that the exercise of power is not restricted to states and bureaucracies, but is part of everyday life. This has resulted in the concerns of political geography increasingly overlapping with those of other human geography sub-disciplines such as economic geography, and, particularly, with those of social and cultural geography in relation to the study of the politics of place. Although contemporary political geography maintains many of its traditional concerns the multi-disciplinary expansion into related areas is part of a general process within human geography which involves the blurring of boundaries between formerly discrete areas of study, and through which the discipline as a whole is enriched.

References

Agnew J., *Political geography: a reader,* London: Arnold, 1997.

Buleon P., 'The state of political geography in France in the 1970s and 1980s', *Progress in Human Geography,* Vol. 16 (1), 1992.

Burbank M.J., "The psychological basis of contextual effects", *Political Geography* 14 (6-7), 1995.

Butler, David L., "Technogeopolitics and the struggle for control of world air routes, 1910-1928", *Political Geography* 20 (5), 2001.

Byron J., "Globalization and Neoliberalism: The Caribbean Context", *Political Geography* 18 (7), 1999.

Carmines E.G., R. Huckfeldt, C. McCurley, "Mobilization, counter-mobilization and the politics of race", *Political Geography,* 14 (6-7), 1995.

Carter S.K., "The Rise and Fall of State Socialism", *Political Geography,* 17 (8), 1998.

Chan S., "Ethics and International Relations", *Political Geography,* 17 (6), 1998.

Chopra J., "The space of peace-maintenance", *Political Geography,* 15 (3-4), 1996.

Christiansen T., "Creating Boundaries: The Politics of Race and Nation", *Political Geography,* 17 (8), 1998.

Feenberg A., *"Critical Theory of Technology"*, SFU. 22 May, 2006.

Harvey D., *Justice, nature and the geography of difference,* Oxford: Blackwell, 1996

Johnston R.J., *Political, electoral and spatial systems,* Oxford: Clarendon Press, 1979

Painter J., *Politics, geography and 'political geography': a critical perspective,* London: Arnold, 1995.

Pepper D., *Modern environmentalism,* London: Routledge, 1996.

Sack R.D., *Human territoriality: its theory and history,* Cambridge: Cambridge University Press, 1986.

Short J.R., *An introduction to political geography,* 2nd edn., London: Routledge, 1993.

Taylor P.J., *Political geography: world economy, nation state and locality,* Harlow: Longman Scientific & Technical, 1993.

7

Population Geography

7.1. Introduction

Population geography involves demography in a geographical perspective. It focuses on the characteristics of population distributions that change in a spatial context. Examples can be shown through population density maps. A few types of maps that show the spatial layout of population are chloropleth, isoline, and dot maps.

7.2. Immigration

Immigration is the movement of people from one nation-state to another. While human migration has existed throughout human history, immigration implies long-term permanent residence (and often eventual citizenship) by the immigrants: tourists and short-term visitors are not considered immigrants. However, seasonal labour migration is often treated as a form of immigration.

The modern idea of immigration is related to the development of nation-states and nationality law. Citizenship of a nation-state confers an inalienable right of residence in thatsigration law. The nation-state made immigration a political issue: by definition it is the homeland of a nation defined by shared ethnicity and/or culture, and in most cases immigrants have a different ethnicity and culture. This has led to social tensions, xenophobia, and conflicts about national identity, in many developed countries. Illegal immigration refers to immigration across national borders in a way that violates the immigration laws of the destination country. Under this definition, an illegal immigrant is a foreigner who either illegally crossed an international political border, be it by land, sea or air, or a foreigner who legally entered a country but nevertheless overstay their visa in order to live and/or work therein.

7.2.1. Theories of Immigration

Theories of immigration traditionally distinguish between push factors and pull factors. Push factors refer primarily to the motive for emigration from the country of origin. In the case of economic migration, differentials in wage rates are prominent. Poor individuals from less developed countries can have far higher standards of living in developed countries than in their originating countries. Escape from poverty is a traditional push factor, the availability of jobs is the related pull factor. Natural disasters and overpopulation can amplify poverty-driven migration flows. This kind of migration may be illegal immigration in the destination country.

Emigration and immigration are sometimes mandatory in a contract of employment: religious missionaries, and employees of transnational corporations, international non-governmental organisations and the diplomatic service can expect to work 'overseas'. They are often referred to as 'expatriates', and their conditions of employment are typically equal to or better than those applying in the host country.

For some migrants, education is the primary pull factor. Retirement migration from rich countries to lower-cost countries with better climate, is a new type of international migration. An example is immigration of retired British citizens to Spain or Italy.

Some, although relatively few, immigrants justify their drive to be in a different country for cultural or health related reasons and very seldom, again in relative quantitative terms compared to the actual number of international migrants worldwide, choose to migrate as a form of self-expression towards the establishment or to satisfy their need to directly perceive other cultural environments because economics is almost always the primary motivator for constant, long-term, or permanent migration, but especially for that type of inter-regional or inter-continental migration; that holds true even for people from developed countries.

Non-economic push factors include persecution (religious and otherwise), frequent abuse, bullying, oppression, ethnic cleansing and even genocide, and risks to civilians during war. Political motives traditionally motivate refugee flows—to escape dictatorship for instance.

Some migration is for personal reasons, based on a relationship (e.g. to be with family or a partner). In a few cases, an individual may wish to emigrate to a new country in a form of transferred patriotism. Evasion of criminal justice is a (mostly negative) personal motivation. This type of emigration and immigration is not normally legal, if a crime is internationally recognised, although criminals may disguise their identities or find other loopholes to evade detection. There have been cases, for example, of those who might be guilty of war crimes disguising themselves as victims of war or conflict and then pursuing asylum in a different country.

Barriers to immigration come not only in legal form; natural barriers to immigration can also be very powerful. Immigrants when leaving their country also leave everything familiar: their family, friends, support network, and culture. They also need to liquidate their assets often at a large cost, and incur the expense of moving. When they arrive in a new country this is often with many uncertainties including finding work, where to live, new laws, new cultural norms, language or accent issues, possible racism and other exclusionary behaviour towards them and their family. These barriers act to limit international migration: scenarios where populations move *en masse* to other continents, creating huge population surges, and their associated strain on infrastructure and services, ignore these inherent limits on migration.

Immigration is often highly politicised, and in some countries, a major political issue. Opposition to immigration is generally far more prominent than support for it, but that is to some extent countered by economic interests.

Immigration policies which selectively grant freedom of movement to targeted individuals are intended to produce a net economic gain for the host country. They can also mean net loss for a poor donor country through the loss of the educated minority—the brain drain. This can exacerbate the global inequality in standards of living that provided the motivation for the individual to migrate in the first place. An example of the 'competition for skilled labour' is active recruitment of health workers by First World countries, from the Third World.

7.3. Human Migration

Human migration denotes any movement by humans from one locality to another, often over long distances or in large groups. Humans are known to have migrated extensively throughout history and prehistory.

Migration and population isolation is one of the four evolutionary forces (along with natural selection, genetic drift, and mutation). The movement of populations in modern times has continued under the form of both voluntary migration within one's region, country, or beyond, and involuntary migration (which includes slave trade, Trafficking in human beings and ethnic cleansing). The people who migrate are called migrants, or, more specifically, emigrants, immigrants or settlers, depending on historical setting, circumstance and perspective.

Human migration has taken place at all times and in the greatest variety of circumstances. It has been tribal, national, class and individual. Its causes have been climatic, political, economic, religious, or more love of adventure. Its causes and results are fundamental for the study of ethnology, of political and social history, and of political economy.

The pressures of human migrations, whether as outright conquest or by slow cultural infiltration and resettlement, have affected the grand epochs in history; under the form of colonisation, migration has transformed the world. Population genetics studied in traditionally settled modern populations have opened a window into the historical patterns of migrations, a technique pioneered by Luigi Luca Cavalli-Sforza.

Forced migration has been a means of social control under authoritarian regimes, yet under free initiative migration is a powerful factor in social adjustment (e.g. the growth of urban populations).

7.3.1. Push and Pull Factors

Push and Pull factors are those factors which either forcefully push someone into migration or attract them. A push factor is a forceful factor, and a factor which relates to the country the person is migrating from. It is generally a problem which the results in people wanting to migrate. Different types of push factors can be seen further below. A pull factor is something concerning the country a person migrates to. It is generally a good thing that attracts people to a certain place. Push and Pull factors are usually considered as north and south poles on a magnet. The idea is to have the attraction in the middle, i.e the place.

7.4. Modern Migrations

7.4.1. Industrialisation

While the pace of migration had accelerated since the 18th century already, it would increase further in the 19th century. Manning distinguishes three major types of migration: labour migration, refugee migrations and lastly: urbanisation. Millions of agricultural workers left the countryside and moved to the cities causing unprecedented levels of urbanisation. This phenomenon began in Britain in the late 18th century and spread around the world and continues to this day in many areas.

Industrialisation encouraged migration wherever it appeared. The increasingly global economy globalised the labour market. Atlantic slave trade diminished sharply after 1820, which gave rise to self-bound contract labour migration from Europe and Asia to plantations. Also overpopulation, open agricultural frontiers and rising industrial centres attracted voluntary, encouraged and sometimes coerced migration. Moreover, migration was significantly eased by improved transportation techniques.

7.4.2. Migrations and Climate Cycles

The modern field of climate history suggests that the successive waves of Eurasian nomadic movement throughout history have had their origins in climatic cycles, which have expanded or contracted pasture land in Central Asia, especially Mongolia and the Altai. People were displaced from their home ground by other tribes trying to find land that could be grazed by essential flocks, each group pushing the next further to the south and west, into the highlands of Anatolia, the plains of Hungary, into Mesopotamia or southwards, into the rich pastures of China.

7.4.3. Emigration

Emigration is the act and the phenomenon of leaving one's native country to settle in another country. It is the same as immigration but from the perspective of the country of origin. Human movement before the establishment of state boundaries or within one state, is termed migration. There are many reasons why people might choose to emigrate. Some are for political or economic reasons, or for personal reasons like finding a spouse while visiting another country and emigrating to be with them. Many older people living in rich nations with cold climates will choose to move to warmer climates when they retire.

Many political or economic emigrants move together with their families toward new regions or new countries where they hope to find peace or job opportunities not available to them in their original location. Throughout history a large number of emigrants return to their homelands, often after they have earned sufficient money in the other country. Sometimes these emigrants move to countries with big cultural differences and will always feel as guests in their destinations, and preserve their original culture, traditions and language, sometimes transmitting them to their children. The conflict between the native and the newer culture may easily create social contrasts, generally resulting in an uncomfortable situation for the "foreigners", who have to understand legal and social systems sometimes new and strange to them. Often, communities of emigrants grow up in the destination areas.

Emigration had a profound influence on the world in the 19th and the 20th century, when hundreds of thousands of poor families left Europe for the United States, Canada, Brazil, Argentina, Australia and New Zealand.

Even though definitions may be vague and vary somewhat, emigration/immigration should not be confused with the phenomenon of involuntary migration, such as instances of population transfer or ethnic cleansing.

7.5. Overpopulation

Overpopulation is a condition when an organism's numbers exceed the carrying capacity of its ecological niche. In common parlance, the term usually refers to the relationship between the human population and its environment, the Earth.

Overpopulation is not simply a function of the size or density of the population. Overpopulation can be determined using the ratio of population to available resources. If a given environment has a population of ten, but there is food or drinking water enough for only nine, then that environment is overpopulated; if the population is 100 individuals but there is food, shelter or water enough for 200, then it is not. Overpopulation can result from an increase in births, a decline in mortality rates due to medical advances, from an increase in immigration, a decrease in emigration, or from an unsustainable use and depletion of resources. It is possible for very sparsely-populated areas to be "overpopulated", as the area in question may have a very meager or non-existent capability to sustain human life.

The resources to be considered when evaluating whether an ecological niche is overpopulated include clean water, clean air, food, shelter, warmth, and other resources necessary to sustain life. If the quality of human life is addressed as well, there are then additional resources to be considered, such as medical care, employment, money, education, fuel, electricity, proper sewage treatment, waste management, and transportation. Negative impacts should also be considered including crowding stress and increased pollution. If addressing the environment as a whole, the survival and well-being of species other than humans must also be considered.

In the context of human societies, overpopulation occurs when the population density is so great as to actually cause an impaired quality of life, serious environmental degradation, or long-term shortages of essential goods and services. This is the definition used by popular dictionaries such Merriam-Webster. Overpopulation is not merely an imbalance between the number of individuals compared to the resources needed for survival, or a ratio of population over resources, or a function of the number or density of individuals, compared to the resources they need to survive.

Some countries have managed to increase their carrying capacity by using technologies such as agriculture, desalination, and nuclear power. Some people have argued that poverty and famine are caused by bad government and bad economic policies, and that higher population density leads to more specialisation and technological innovation, and that this leads to a higher standard of living.

In an *Essay on the Principle of Population,* Thomas Malthus proposed that while resources tend to grow linearly, population grows exponentially. He argued that, if left unrestricted, human populations continue to grow until they would become too large to be supported by the food grown on available agricultural land, causing starvation which then controls population growth. He argued that this had happened many times previously in human history and estimated that this would occur again by the middle of the 19th century. To avoid this happening, Malthus argued for population control through "moral restraint". While arguably he was right about human history up to his time, he made his prediction for the future exactly at the time the industrial revolution and a similar revolution in agriculture caused a very large increase in available resources. His specific predictions therefore failed because he used a static analysis, and extrapolated his historical numbers into the future without considering factors that could increase the resource base available to humanity faster than he thought, or factors which cause population growth to decline or reverse.

On a global scale, since the industrial revolution, food production has grown faster than human population. However, it has been argued that other changes impacting earth's ability to function as a suitable habitat for human beings, such as global warming, desertification, overfishing and other environmental problems caused by industrialisation, will eventually affect food production or factors necessary for well-being. Along with continued population growth, this may cause a Malthusian catastrophe.

David Pimentel claims that population outcomes for the 22nd century range from 2 billion people, to 12 billion people (characterised as miserable and suffering difficult lives with limited resources and widespread famine).

Julian Simon predicted that any poor country that chose to adopt property rights, science, technology, industrialisation, modern agriculture, hydroponic farming, nuclear power, and desalination, would achieve a rich, first world standard of living, even if the earth had tens of billions of people. However, Simon's predictions about the earth being able to support quadrillions of people have been criticised by Hardin, Bartlett, Diamond and others.

Between 1950 and 1984, as the Green Revolution transformed agriculture around the globe, world grain production increased by 250%. The energy for the Green Revolution was provided by fossil fuels in the form of fertilisers (natural gas), pesticides (oil), and hydrocarbon fuelled irrigation. David Pimentel, professor of ecology and agriculture at Cornell University, and Mario Giampietro, senior researcher at the National Research Institute on Food and Nutrition (INRAN), place in theirs study Food, Land, Population and the U.S. Economy the maximum U.S. population for a sustainable economy at 200 million.

7.6. Population Growth

7.6.1. Theory of Demographic Transition

The theory of demographic transition, while unproven to apply to all world regions, holds that within a generation after the standard of living and life expectancy increases, family sizes start dropping. Factors cited in the decline of birth rates include such social factors as later ages of marriage, the growing desire of many women in such settings to seek careers outside of child rearing and domestic work, and the decreased need of children in industrialised settings. The latter factor stems from the fact that children perform a great deal of work in small-scale agricultural societies, and work less in industrial ones; it has been cited to explain the dropoff in birth rates worldwide in all industrialising regions.

Another version of demographic transition is that of Virginia Abernethy in Population Politics, in which she claims that the demographic transition is primarily in effect for nations where women enjoy a special status. In strongly patriarchal nations, where she claims women enjoy few special rights, a high standard of living tends to result in population growth. She argues that foreign aid to poor countries must include significant components designed to improve the education, human rights, political rights, political power, and also to equalise the economic and sexual status and power of women.

"Demographic entrapment" is a concept developed by Maurice King that has not gained widespread acceptance. King argues that this occurs when a country has a population larger than its carrying capacity, no possibility of migration, and exports too little to be able to import food. This will cause starvation. He claims that for example many sub-Saharan nations are or will become stuck in demographic entrapment, instead of having a demographic transition.

A comparison of fertility rates in Italy and Sweden suggest Italy is alleviating overpopulation more than Sweden due primarily to greater gender inequality and fewer social services, similar findings from the same source relate to Japan, Russia and Estonia. First and second world effects of social services and gender equality on overpopulation appear to be the opposite of those found in the third world.

7.6.1.1. Birth control

Overpopulation is also related to issues of birth control, with some nations like China using strict measures in order to reduce birth rates, while religious and ideological opposition to birth control has been cited as a factor contributing to overpopulation and poverty. There are an estimated 350 million women in the poorest countries of the world who either did not want their last child, do not want another child or want to space their pregnancies, but they lack access to information, affordable means and services to determine the size and spacing of their families. In the developing world, some 514,000 women die of complications from pregnancy and abortion on a yearly basis. Additionally, 8 million infants die, many because of malnutrition or preventable diseases.

David Pimentel, Professor Emeritus at Cornell University, has stated that "With the imbalance growing between population numbers and vital life sustaining resources, humans must actively conserve cropland, freshwater, energy, and biological resources. There is a need to develop renewable energy resources. Humans everywhere must understand that rapid population growth damages the earth's resources and diminishes human well being."

Some writers such as Julian Simon and Bjorn Lomborg and many of a conservative libertarian persuasion, on the other hand, believe that resources abound for a furtherance of population growth. And population scientists have agreed with their assessments that there are indeed more resources left that would enable continued population growth. A large expansion of agriculture to provide growing populations with improved diets is likely to lead to further deforestation, loss of species, soil erosion, and pollution from pesticides and fertiliser runoff as farming intensifies and new land is brought into production".

Additionally, other issues involving quality of life—would most people want to live in a world of tens of billions of people—and the basic right of other species to exist in their native environments come into play.

Worldwide, the number of people who are overweight has surpassed the number who are malnourished. In a 2006 news story, MSNBC reported, "There are an estimated 800 million undernourished people and more than a billion considered overweight worldwide." Water deficits, which are already spurring heavy grain imports in numerous smaller countries, may soon do the same in larger countries, such as China or India. The water tables are falling in scores of countries (including Northern China, the US, and India) due to widespread overpumping using powerful diesel and electric pumps. Other countries affected include Pakistan, Iran, and Mexico. This will eventually lead to water scarcity and cutbacks in grain harvest. Even with the overpumping of its aquifers, China is developing a grain deficit. When this happens, it will almost certainly drive grain prices upward.

Most of the 3 billion people projected to be added worldwide by mid-century will be born in countries already experiencing water shortages. Unless population growth can be slowed quickly by investing heavily in female literacy and family planning services, there may not be a humane solution to the emerging world water shortage. Desalination is a real world, humane solution to the problem of water shortages, although probably not effective.

After China and India, there is a second tier of smaller countries with large water deficits—Algeria, Egypt, Iran, Mexico, and Pakistan. Four of these already import a large share of their grain. Only Pakistan remains self-sufficient. But with a population expanding by 4 million a year, it will also likely soon turn to the world market for grain.

The famine in Zimbabwe was caused by government seizure of farmland. However drought has also played a major role. "Well, the United Nations statistics are saying that thirteen-million people are threatened by famine, in light of the drought in southern Africa. Six-million of them live in Zimbabwe. So that is a contingent of fully half of those potentially threatened by the current food shortages, if indeed they get worse, as is projected". Prior to this combination of drought and seizure of farmland, Zimbabwe had been exporting so much food that it was called "the breadbasket of southern Africa." So other countries were also harmed by these farm seizures. People who study the Zimbabwean famine claim that normally there are more than enough natural resources to feed the people. Some claim that the dams and rivers in Zimbabwe are full, and that the famine has nothing to do with drought.

Thinkers such as David Pimentel, a professor from Cornell University, Virginia Abernethy, Alan Thornhill, Russell Hopffenberg and author Daniel Quinn propose that like any animals, human populations predictably grow and shrink according to their available food supply—populations grow in an abundance of food, and shrink in times of scarcity.

Proponents of this theory argue that every time food production is increased, the population grows. Some human populations throughout history support this theory. Populations of hunter-gatherers fluctuate in accordance with the amount of available food. Population increased after the Neolithic Revolution and an increased food supply. This was followed by subsequent population growth after subsequent agricultural revolutions.

Critics of this idea point out that birth rates are lowest in the developed nations, which also has the highest access to food. In fact, some developed countries have both a diminishing population and an abundant food supply. The United Nations projects that the population of 51 countries or areas, including Germany, Italy, Japan and most of the successor states of the former Soviet Union, is expected to be lower in 2050 than in 2005. This shows that human populations do not always grow to match the available food supply; also, many of these countries are major exporters of food.

Despite advances in agriculture, the fresh water supplies that it depends on are running low worldwide. Some argue that this water crisis is only expected to worsen as the population increases. Lester R. Brown of the Earth Policy Institute argues that declining water supplies could well have future disastrous consequences for agriculture.

However, the amount of freshwater is not necessarily limited to what is currently available in nature. Malta derives two thirds of its freshwater from desalination of salt water. This is an energy intensive process. One possible solution is large expansion of nuclear powered desalination plants. Such plants already exist. Some argue that there are billions of years of nuclear fuel available. Critics point to the high costs of desalination technologies, especially for poor third world countries, the impracticability and cost of transporting or piping massive amounts of desalinated seawater throughout the interiors of large countries, and the "lethal byproduct of saline brine that is a major cause of marine pollution when dumped back into the oceans at high temperatures."

One study of the costs of desalination and its transport says that "Indeed, one needs to lift the water by 2000 m, or transport it over more than 1600 km to get transport costs equal to the desalination costs. Thus, desalinated water is very expensive only in places far from the sea, like New Delhi, or in high places, like Mexico City. Desalinated water is also expensive in places that are both somewhat far from the sea and somewhat high, such as Riyadh and Harare. Newer agricultural technologies do not always require more water usage; for example hydroponics and green houses require less.

7.6.1.2. Land

World Resources Institute states that "Agricultural conversion to croplands and managed pastures has affected some 3.3 billion [hectares]—roughly 26 percent of the land area. All totalled, agriculture has displaced one-third of temperate and tropical forests and one-quarter of natural grasslands". Energy development may also require large areas, like for hydroelectric dams. Usable land may become less useful through salinisation or desertification. Global warming may cause flooding of many of the most productive agricultural areas. Thus, available useful land may become a limiting factor.

High crop yield vegetables like potatoes and lettuce do not waste space with inedible plant parts, like stalks, husks, vines, and inedible leaves. New varieties of selectively bred and hybrid plants have larger edible parts (fruit, vegetable, grain) and smaller inedible parts; however, many of the gains of agricultural technology are now historic, with new advances being more difficult to achieve. With new technologies, it is possible to grow crops on some marginal land under certain conditions. Aquaculture could theoretically increase available area. Hydroponics and food from bacteria and fungi, like Quorn, may allow the growing of food without having to consider land quality, climate, or even available sunlight, although such a process may be very energy-intensive.

Some claim that not all arable land will remain productive if used for agriculture, as they argue that some marginal land can only be made to produce food by unsustainable practices like slash-and-burn agriculture. Even with the modern techniques of agriculture, the sustainability of production is in question.

Some scientists have said that in the future, densely populated cities will use vertical farming to grow food inside skyscrapers.

Some countries, such as Dubai have constructed large artificial islands, or have created large dam and dike systems, like the Netherlands, which reclaim land from the water to increase their total land area.

7.6.1.3. Energy

Enthusiasts have also been criticised for failing to account for future shortages in fossil fuels, currently used for fertiliser and transportation for modern agriculture. They counter that there will be enough fossil fuels until suitable replacement technologies have been developed, for example hydrogen in a hydrogen economy.

There has also been increasing development in renewable energy resources, such as solar, wind, and tidal energy, which, if used on a wide scale, could supplement most, if not all, of the energy needs currently being filled by non-renewable resources. However, it should be noted that some of these renewable resources also have ecological footprints, though they may be different or smaller than some non-renewable resources.

7.6.1.4. Fertiliser

Modern agriculture uses large amounts of fertiliser. Since much of this fertiliser is made from petroleum, the problem of peak oil is of concern. According to a 2003 article in Discover magazine, it is possible to use the process of thermal depolymerisation to manufacture fertiliser out of garbage, sewage, and agricultural waste.

7.6.1.5. Wealth and poverty

The United Nations indicates that about 850 million people are malnourished or starving, and 1.1 billion people do not have access to safe drinking water. Thus some argue that the Earth may support 6 billion people, but only on the condition that many live in misery. Others posit that poverty was worse in the past when the population was smaller, and that worldwide poverty is declining as the population grows. The percentage of the world's population living on less than $1 per day has halved in twenty years; these are inflation adjusted numbers. Furthermore, a 2007 article from Investor's Business Daily suggests that the population explosion has been accompanied by an increase in worldwide living standards.

However states the UN Human Development Report from 1997 "During the last 15-20 years, more than 100 developing countries, and several East European countries, have suffered from disastrous growth failures. The reductions in standard of living have been deeper and more long-lasting than what was seen in the industrialised countries during the depression in the 1930's. As a result, the income for more than one billion people has fallen below the level that was reached 10, 20 or 30 years ago."

North Korea and South Korea have similar population densities and natural resources. But whereas North Korea is a poor, third world country suffering from terrible famine, South Korea is a rich, first world country where the people are well fed. This suggests that it is bad economic policies, not overpopulation, that causes famine. Various Indices of Economic Freedom suggest that countries with a strong level of economic freedom never have famine, no matter how high their population densities become.

7.6.1.6. Clean air

Once a country has industrialised and become wealthy, a combination of government regulation and technological innovation may cause air pollution to decline substantially, even as its population continues to grow. However during that same time period, there were substantial reductions in total annual emissions of carbon monoxide, nitrogen oxides, sulfur dioxide, particulates, and lead.

7.6.1.7. Environment

Overpopulation has had a major impact on the environment of Earth starting at least as early as the 20th century. Many posit that the human population has expanded, enabled by over-exploiting natural resources, with resultant adverse impacts upon biodiversity, aquifer sustainability, climate change and even human health. There are also indirect economic consequences of this environmental degradation in the form of ecosystem services attrition. Beyond the scientifically verifiable harm to the environment, some argue the moral right of other species to simply exist, protected from human exploitation.

Some people claim that the problems of nuclear waste do not come anywhere close to approaching the problems of fossil fuel waste. Three million people are killed worldwide by outdoor air pollution annually from vehicles and industrial emissions, and 1.6 million indoors through using solid fuel. In the U.S. alone, fossil fuel waste kills 20,000 people each year. A coal power plant releases 100 times as much radiation as a nuclear power plant of the same wattage. In addition, fossil fuel waste causes global warming, which leads to increased deaths from hurricanes, flooding, and other weather events.

7.6.1.8. Cities

In 1800 only 3% of the world's population lived in cities. By the 20th century's close, 47% did so. In 1950, there were 83 cities with populations exceeding one million; but by 2007, this had risen to 468 agglomerations of more than one million. If the trend continues, the world's urban population will double every 38 years, say researchers. The UN forecasts that today's urban population of 3.2 billion will rise to nearly 5 billion by 2030, when three out of five people will live in cities.

The increase will be most dramatic in the poorest and least-urbanised continents, Asia and Africa. Surveys and projections indicate that all urban growth over the next 25 years will be in developing countries. One billion people, one-sixth of the world's population, or one-third of urban population, now live in shanty towns, which are seen as "breeding grounds" for social problems such as crime, drug addiction, alcoholism, poverty and unemployment. In many poor countries slums exhibit high rates of disease due to unsanitary conditions, malnutrition, and lack of basic health care. By 2030, over 2 billion people in the world will be living in slums.

India also has enormous problems with overpopulation. The current population is over a billion, but India does not have much land mass such as China. India is experiencing major problems with declining water tables due to over-extraction beyond sustainable yield. India is building desalination plants to solve this problem. Because India has the same population density as Japan, some have claimed that India's poverty is caused by underdevelopment, not overpopulation.

7.7. Illegal Immigration

Illegal immigration refers to immigration across national borders in a way that violates the immigration laws of the destination country. Under this definition, an illegal immigrant is a foreigner who either has illegally crossed an international political border, be it by land, sea or air, or a foreigner who has entered a country legally but then overstays his/her visa in order to live and/or work therein. In politics, the term may imply a larger set of social issues and time constraints with disputed consequences in areas such as economy, social welfare, education, health care, slavery, prostitution, crime, legal protections, voting rights, public services, and human rights. Illegal emigration would be leaving a country in a manner that violates the laws of the country being exited.

7.7.1. Causes

7.7.1.1. War

One motive of illegal immigration is to escape civil war or repression in the country of origin. Non-economic push factors include persecution (religious and otherwise), frequent abuse, bullying, oppression, ethnic cleansing and even genocide, and risks to civilians during war. Political motives traditionally motivate refugee flows—to escape dictatorship for instance.

7.7.1.2. Family reunion

Some illegal immigrants seek to live with loved ones, such as a spouse or other family members. This is particularly true for the families of binational same sex couples. The Lesbian and Gay Immigration Rights Task Force (LGIRTF) warns binational same sex couples in the US that marriage may actually increase the likelihood of becoming undocumented, rather than decreasing it. Other individuals seek to distance themselves from their spouses.

7.7.1.3. Poverty

Another reason for illegal immigration is to escape poverty. Natural disasters and overpopulation can amplify poverty-driven migration flows. According to CBS 60 Minutes, U.S. Marine Lance Corporal Jose Gutierrez, one of the first U.S. servicemen to die in combat in Iraq, a former street child in Guatemala having been orphaned at age 8, first entered the US as an illegal immigrant in 1997 to escape poverty, and dreamed of being an architect. Sometimes the person moves over the border because the wage-labour ratio is much higher in the neighbouring country, as is the case with the US illegal immigration.

7.7.1.4. Prostitution and slavery

Illegal immigrants may also be trafficked. After the end of the legal international slave trade by the European nations and the

United States in the early 19th century, the illegal importation of slaves has continued, albeit at much reduced levels. Although not as common as in Europe, Asia, Africa and Latin America, some women are undoubtedly smuggled into the United States and Canada. The so-called "white slave trade" referred to the smuggling of women, almost always under duress or fraud, for the purposes of forced prostitution. Now more generically called "sexual slavery" it continues to be a problem, particularly in Eastern Europe and the Middle East, though there has been an increase in the number of cases in the U.S. People may also be kidnapped or tricked into slavery to work as labourers, for example in factories. Those trafficked in this manner often face additional barriers to escaping slavery, since their status as illegal immigrants makes it difficult for them to gain access to help or services. For example Burmese women trafficked into Thailand and forced to work in factories or as prostitutes may not speak the language and may be vulnerable to abuse by police due to their illegal immigrant status.

In the Dominican Republic, Haitian migrant workers are sold into slavery on Dominican Sugar plantations, including children. Some Haitian children have allegedly been forced to work as prostitutes in the Dominican sexual tourism industry. Currently the Dominican sex trade ranks third in the world, only behind Thailand and the Philippines.

7.7.2. Methods

7.7.2.1. Border crossing

Immigrants from nations that do not have an automatic visa agreements, or who would not otherwise qualify for a visa, often cross the borders illegally in some areas like the United States-Mexico border, the Mona Channel between the Dominican Republic and Puerto Rico, the Strait of Gibraltar, Fuerteventura, and the Strait of Otranto. Because these methods are illegal, they are often dangerous. Would-be immigrants suffocate in shipping containers, boxcars, and trucks, sink in shipwrecks caused by unseaworthy vessels, die of dehydration or exposure during long walks without water.

Human smuggling is the practice of intermediaries aiding illegal immigrants in crossing over international borders in financial gain, often in large groups. Human smuggling differs from, but is sometimes associated with, human trafficking. A human smuggler will facilitate illegal entry into a country for a fee, but on arrival at their destination, the smuggled person is usually free. Trafficking involves a process of using physical force, fraud, or deception to obtain and transport people.

7.7.2.2. Overstays

Some illegal immigrants enter a country legally and then overstay or violate their visa. A related way of becoming an illegal immigrant is through bureaucratic means. For example, a person can be allowed to remain in a country—or be protected from expulsion—because he/she needs special pension for a medical condition, etc., without being able to regularise his/her situation and obtain a work and/or residency permit, let alone naturalisation. Hence, categories of people being neither illegal immigrants nor legal citizens are created, living in a judicial "no man's land".

7.7.3. Legal and Political Status

Many countries have had or currently have laws restricting immigration for economic or nationalistic political reasons. Whether a person is permitted to stay in a country legally may be decided by quotas or point systems or may be based on considerations such as family ties (marriage, elderly mother, etc.). Exceptions relative to political refugees or to sick people are also common. Immigrants who do not participate in these legal proceedings or who are denied permission under them and still enter or stay in the country are illegal immigrants.

Most countries have laws requiring workers to have proper documentation, often intended to prevent or minimise the employment of unauthorised immigrants. However the penalties against employers are often small and the acceptable identification requirements vague and ill-defined as well as being seldom checked or enforced, making it easy for employers to hire unauthorised labour. Unauthorised immigrants are especially popular with many employers because they can pay less than the legal minimum wage or have unsafe working conditions, secure in the knowledge that few unauthorised workers will report the abuse to the authorities. Often the minimum wages in one country can be several times the prevailing wage in the unauthorised immigrant's country, making even these jobs attractive to the unauthorised worker.

The right to freedom of movement of an individual within National borders is often contained within the constitution or in a country's human rights legislation but these rights are restricted to citizens and exclude all others. Some argue that the freedom of movement both within and between countries is a basic human right and that nationalism and immigration policies of state governments violate this human right that those same governments recognise within their own borders. According to the Universal Declaration of Human Rights, fundamental human rights are violated when citizens are forbidden to leave their country.

Since illegal immigrants without proper legal status have no valid identification documents such as identity cards, they may have reduced or no access to public health systems, proper housing, education and banks. This lack of access may result in the creation or expansion of illegal underground forgery to provide this documentation. When the authorities are overwhelmed in their efforts to stop illegal immigration, they have historically provided amnesty. Amnesties, which are becoming less tolerated by the citizenry, waive the "subject to deportation" clause associated with illegal aliens.

7.7.4. Multinational Corporation

A multinational corporation (MNC) is a corporation or enterprise that manages production establishments or delivers services in at least two countries. Very large multinationals have budgets that exceed those of many countries. Multinational corporations can have a powerful influence in international relations and local economies. Multinational corporations play an important role in globalisation; some argue that a new form of MNC is evolving in response to globalisation-e.g. the 'globally integrated enterprise'.

7.7.4.1. International Power

Large multinational corporations can have a powerful influence in international relations, given their large economic influence in politicians' representative districts, as well as their extensive financial resources available for public relations and political lobbying.

Multinationals have played an important role in globalisation. Prospective country locations for MNC production establishments, and sometimes regions within countries, must compete with each other to have MNCs locate their facilities (and subsequent tax revenue, employment, and economic activity) within a region. To compete, countries and regional political districts offer incentives to MNCs such as tax breaks, pledges of governmental assistance or improved infrastructure, or lax environmental and labour standards. This process of becoming more attractive to foreign investment can be characterised as a race to the bottom, a push towards greater freedom for corporate bodies, or both.

An inaccurate claim is that out of the 100 largest economies in the world, 51 are multinational corporations. This claim is based on a miscalculation, where two numbers describing totally different things are compared: the GDP of nations to gross sales of corporations. The problem with the comparison is that GDP takes into account only the final value, whereas gross sales don't measure how much was produced outside the company.

Because of their size, multinationals can have a significant impact on government policy, primarily through the threat of market withdrawal. For example, in an effort to reduce health care costs, some countries have tried to force pharmaceutical companies to license their patented drugs to local competitors for a very low fee, thereby artificially lowering the price. When faced with that threat, multinational pharmaceuticals firms have simply withdrawn from the market, which often leads to limited availability of advanced drugs. In those cases, governments have been forced to back down from their efforts. Similar corporate and government confrontations have occurred when governments tried to force companies to make their intellectual property public in an effort to gain technology for local entrepreneurs. When companies are faced with the option of losing their core competitive advantage (technology) and losing a national market, they may choose to withdraw from the national market. This withdrawal often causes governments to change policy. Countries that have been most successful in this type of confrontation with multinational corporations are large countries such as India and Brazil, which have viable indigenous market competitors.

Multinational corporate lobbying is directed at a range of business concerns, from tariff structures to environmental regulations. There is no unified multinational perspective on any of these issues. Companies that have invested heavily in pollution control mechanisms may lobby for very tough environmental standards in an effort to force non-compliant competitors into a weaker position. For every tariff category that one multinational wants to have reduced, there is another multinational that wants the tariff raised. Even within the U.S. auto industry, the fraction of a company's imported components will vary, so some firms favour tighter import restrictions, while others favour looser ones.

In addition to efforts by multinational corporations to affect governments, there are many actions taken by governments to affect corporate behaviour. The threat of nationalisation or changes in local business laws and regulations limit a multinational's power.

The mobility of capital brought by multinational corporations can create "a race to the bottom". This refers to efforts by governments to change their laws and regulations to become more corporate friendly in order to attract multinational investment. As they become more responsive to the interests of multinational corporations, there is the risk that governments can become less responsive to local constituents. Examples of this are laws that bar unionisation or permit lax environmental standards. Those laws are often chosen because governments also find the corporate-friendly rules comfortable.

7.7.4.2. Micro-Multinationals

Enabled by Internet based communication tools, a new breed of multinational companies is growing in numbers. These multinationals start operating in different countries from the very early stages. These companies are being called micro-multinationals. What differentiates micro-multinationals from the large MNCs is the fact that they are still small businesses. Some of the micro-multinationals, particularly software development companies, have been hiring employees in multiple countries from the beginning of the Internet era. But more and more micro-multinationals are actively starting to market their products and services in various countries. Internet giants like Google, Yahoo, MSN, Ebay and Amazon make it a breeze for the micro-multinationals to reach potential customers in other countries.

Contrary to the traditional powerful image of the large MNCs, the micro-multinationals face the limitations and the typical challenges of a small business. In most cases, the micro-multinational companies are being run by technically savvy people who can use various Internet tools to overcome the challenges of remote collaboration, customer service and sales infrastructures.

7.8. Conclusion

Overpopulation arises the potential for catastrophic overshoot. Growth in the globe's population and material economy confronts humanity with this possibility. The potential consequences of this overshoot are profoundly dangerous. The situation is unique; it confronts humanity with a variety of issues never before experienced by our species on a global scale. People lack the perspectives, the cultural norms, the habits, and the institutions required to cope. And the damage will, in many cases, take centuries or millennia to correct. But the consequences need not be catastrophic. People believe that if a profound correction is not made soon, a crash of some sort is certain. And it will occur within the lifetimes of many who are alive today.

References

George A. Schnell and Mark S. Monmonier, *The Study of Population*, 1983.

Gary L. Peters and Robert P. Larkin, *Population Geography*, 2nd ed. 1983.

Huw R. Jones, *A Population Geography*, 1981.

John I. Clarke (ed.), *Geography and Population*, 1984.

Leszek A. Kosínski and R. Mansell Prothero (eds.), *People on the Move: Studies on Internal Migration*, 1975.

Philip M. Hauser (ed.), *World Population and Development*, 1979.

Wilbur Zelinsky, Leszek A. Kosínski, and R. Mansell Prothero (eds.), *Geography and a Crowding World*, 1970.

8

Social Geography

Social geography is the study of how society affects geographical features and how environmental factors affect society.

8.1. Social Geography in India

Victims of their own historical success, Indians suffer from a rural economy. A high population density, poverty and strong echoes of the traditional caste system holds back any progress or urbanisation. The fertile Ganges Valley with monsoon rain and river always supported a dense rural population. Rice is the stable crop. A settled traditional agriculture is practised on small plots, but tenants are exploited by landlords. There is a large mass of landless labourers. Poverty still acute, however, the emerging middle class peasantry benefited from the Green Revolution.

The field of social geography might include the examination of rural exodus or urban exodus or whether low-rise developments generate a different type of daily life than tower blocks.' It deals also with problems of segregation and discrimination, socio-spatial variations in health, analysis of spatial crime patterns and others. In the field of community development, the importance of place has been a focal point for sociologists to determine what effects geography may have on a local community's cohesiveness and the sense of community.

8.1.1. Rural Exodus

Rural exodus is a term used to describe the migratory patterns that normally occur in a region following the mechanisation of agriculture. In such a situation, there tends to be a movement of peoples from rural areas into urban areas. This is related to the fact that with mechanisation (or any other change in the method of production which increases productivity) fewer people are needed to bring the same amount of agricultural output to market.

The term is used in the United States especially to describe the flight of people from rural areas in the Great Plains, where, historically, farmers have had difficulties in developing agriculture and have had to migrate to urban areas. An example of this is the Dust Bowl in the 1930s, where people had to flee because of large dust storms. This problem persists to the present day in the western parts of Great Plains states such as Nebraska and Kansas.

Rural flight from the Great Plains has been mentioned in various fiction books, like in John Steinbeck's novel The Grapes of Wrath, in which a family from the Great Plains migrates to California during the Dust Bowl period of the 1930s. The phenomenon of rural flight is also well-known in developing countries, where many people in the countryside live below the poverty line. They migrate to cities to find employment or to get money by begging.

8.1.2. Urban Exodus

When people move to rural areas from large towns and cities, they sometimes have unrealistic expectations of local services (e.g. medical and transport facilities), or do not fit in well with the local culture. The term "urban exodus" has been coined by those who perceive this to be a problem. The definition may also include a form of rural gentrification, in which the presence of wealthier immigrants from more populated areas raises property values and housing prices for long-time residents. While this phenomenon might be beneficial for property owners willing to sell at higher prices, it also tends to raise property taxes and make it more difficult for locals to afford housing (of particular concern to low-income residents and renters).

Rural exodus (or rural flight) is a term used to describe the migratory patterns that normally occur in a region following the mechanisation of agriculture. In such a situation, there tends to be a movement of peoples from rural areas into urban areas. This is related to the fact that with mechanisation (or any other change in the method of production which increases productivity) fewer people are needed to bring the same amount of agricultural output to market.

The term is used in the United States especially to describe the flight of people from rural areas in the Great Plains, where, historically, farmers have had difficulties in developing agriculture and have had to migrate to urban areas. An example of this is the Dust Bowl in the 1930s, where people had to flee because of large dust storms. This problem persists to the present day in the western parts of Great Plains states such as Nebraska and Kansas.

Rural flight from the Great Plains has been mentioned in various fiction books, like in John Steinbeck's novel The Grapes of Wrath, in which a family from the Great Plains migrates to California during the Dust Bowl period of the 1930s.

The phenomenon of rural flight is also well-known in developing countries, where many people in the countryside live below the poverty line. They migrate to cities to find employment or to get money by begging.

8.2. Community Development

Community development, informally called community building, is a broad term applied to the practices and academic disciplines of civic leaders, activists, involved citizens and professionals to improve various aspects of local communities. It may form part of the larger subject of Ecologically Sustainable Community Economic Development (ESCED).

Community development seeks to empower individuals and groups of people by providing these groups with the skills they need to effect change in their own communities. These skills are often concentrated around building political power through the formation of large social groups working for a common agenda. Community developers must understand both how to work with individuals and how to affect communities' positions within the context of larger social institutions.

8.2.1. Community Development Practice

Community development practitioners are involved in organising meetings and conducting searches within a community to identify problems, identify assets, locate resources, analyse local power structures, assess human needs, and investigate other concerns that comprise the community's character. These practitioners, sometimes called social activists, use social resources to get the economic and political leverage that a community uses to meet their needs. Often, the social resources within the community are found to be adequate to meet these needs if individuals work collectively through techniques like cooperation and volunteerism.

A form of community development that links academic resources to community problems in a reciprocally beneficial manner is community-based participatory research (CBPR), a form of research which engages a community fully in the process of problem definition/issue selection, research design, conducting research, and interpreting the results. One of the principal ways in which CBPR differs from traditional research is that instead of creating knowledge for the advancement of a field or for knowledge's sake, CBPR is an iterative process, incorporating research, reflection, and action in a cyclical process. In the UK Rural Community Councils support local communities to build sustainable futures. They assist local communities in a form of CBPR called community led planning. Rural Community Councils employ experienced, independent community development workers.

Community Development has been a sometimes explicit, sometimes implicit goal of community people, aiming to achieve, through collective effort, a better life, and has occurred throughout history. In the 18th Century the work of the early socialist thinker Robert Owen, sought through Community Planning, to create the perfect community. At New Lanark and at later utopian communities such as Oneida in the USA and the New Australia Movement in Australia, groups of people came together to create intentional utopian communities, with mixed success. Such community planning techniques became important in the 1920s and 1930s in East Africa, where Community Development proposals were seen as a way of helping local people improve their own lives with indirect assistance from colonial authorities.

Mohondas K. Gandhi adopted African community development ideals as a basis of his South African Ashram, and then introduced it as a part of the Indian Swaraj movement, aiming at establishing economic interdependence at village level throughout India. With Indian independence, despite the continuing work of Vinoba Bhave in encouraging grassroots land reform, India under its first Prime Minister Jawaharlal Nehru adopted a centralist heavy industry approach, antithetical to self-help community development ideas.

Community Development became a part of the Ujamaa Villages established in Tanzania by Julius Nyerere, where it had some success in assisting with the delivery of education services throughout rural areas, but has elsewhere met with mixed success. In the 1970s and 1980s, Community Development became a part of "Integrated Rural Development", a strategy promoted by United Nations Agencies and the World Bank.

Community development in Canada has roots in the development of co-operatives, credit unions and caisses populaires. The Antigonish Movement which started in the 1920s in Nova Scotia, through the work of Doctor Moses Coady and Father James Tompkins, has been particularly influential in the subsequent expansion of community economic development work across Canada.

In the 1990s, following critiques of the mixed success of "top down" government programmes, and drawing on the work of Robert Putnam, in the rediscovery of Social Capital, Community Development internationally became concerned with social capital formation. In particular the outstanding success of the work of Muhammad Yunus in Bangladesh with the Grameen Bank, has led to the attempts to spread microenterprise credit schemes around the world. This work was honoured by the 2006 Nobel Peace Prize.

The "Human Scale Development" work of Right Livelihood Award winning Chilean economist Manfred Max Neef promotes the idea of development based upon fundamental human needs, which are considered to be limited, universal and invariant to all human beings. He considers that poverty results from the failure to satisfy a particular human need, it is not just an absence of money. Whilst human needs are limited, Max Neef shows that the ways of satisfying human needs is potentially unlimited. Satisfiers also have different characteristics: they can be violators or destroyers, pseudosatisfiers, inhibiting satisfiers, singular satisfiers, or synergic satisfiers. Max-Neef shows that certain satisfiers, promoted as satisfying a particular need, in fact inhibit or destroy the possibility of satisfying other needs: eg, the arms race, while ostensibly satisfying the need for protection, in fact then destroys subsistence, participation, affection and freedom; formal democracy, which is supposed to meet the need for participation often disempowers and alienates; commercial television, while used to satisfy the need for recreation, interferes with understanding, creativity and identity. Synergic satisfiers, on the other hand, not only satisfy one particular need, but also lead to satisfaction in other areas: some examples are breast-feeding; self-managed production; popular education; democratic community organisations; preventative medicine; meditation; educational games.

8.3. Community Building

Community building is a field of practices directed toward the creation or enhancement of community between individuals within a regional area or with a common interest. It is sometimes encompassed under the field of community development.

A wide variety of practices can be utilised for community building, ranging from simple events like potlucks and small book clubs, to larger-scale efforts such as mass festivals and building construction projects that involve local participants rather than outside contractors. Activists engaged in community building efforts in industrialised nations see the apparent loss of community in these societies as a key cause of social disintegration and the emergence of many harmful behaviours. They may see building community as a means to increase social justice, individual well-being and reduce negative impacts of otherwise disconnected individuals.

Community organising is a process by which people are brought together to act in common self-interest. While organising describes any activity involving people interacting with one another in a formal manner, much community organising is in the pursuit of a common agenda. Many groups seek populist goals and the ideal of participatory democracy. Community organisers create social movements by building a base of concerned people, mobilising these community members to act, and developing leadership from and relationships among the people involved.

8.3.1. Community Economic Development

Community Economic Development (CED) is action taken locally by a community to provide economic opportunities and improve social conditions in a sustainable way. Often CED initiatives aim to improve the lot of those who are disadvantaged. An aspect of "localising economics," CED is a community-centred process that blends social and economic development to foster the economic, social, ecological and cultural well-being of communities.

Community Economic Development is often involved in a process of building Community Enterprises. Sometimes called the Third Sector, a community enterprise is a partnership between government agencies, small to medium enterprises, large national or transnational corporations and the not-for-profit sector, and aims for social, economic and/or environmental outcomes that none of these agencies could achieve for and by themselves.

8.3.2. Sense of Community

Sense of community (or psychological sense of community) is a concept in social psychology, which focuses on the experience of community rather than its structure, formation, setting, or other features. Sociologists, social psychologists, anthropologists, and others have theorised about and carried out empirical research on community, but the psychological approach asks questions about the individual's perception, understanding, attitudes, feelings, etc. about community and his or her relationship to it and to others' participation - indeed to the complete, multifaceted community experience.

In his seminal 1974 book, psychologist Seymour B. Sarason proposed that Psychological Sense of Community become the conceptual center for the psychology of community, asserting that it "is one of the major bases for self-definition." By 1986 it was regarded as a central overarching concept for Community Psychology.

For Sarason, Psychological Sense of Community is "the perception of similarity to others, an acknowledged interdependence with others, a willingness to maintain this interdependence by giving to or doing for others what one expects from them, and the feeling that one is part of a larger dependable and stable structure."

McMillan & Chavis define Sense of Community as "a feeling that members have of belonging, a feeling that members matter to one another and to the group, and a shared faith that members' needs will be met through their commitment to be together."

Gusfield identified two dimensions of community, territorial and relational. The relational dimension of community has to do with the nature and quality of relationships in that community, and some communities may even have no discernible territorial demarcation, as in the case of a community of scholars working in a particular speciality, who have some kind of contact and quality of relationship, but may live and work in disparate locations, perhaps even throughout the world. Other communities may seem to be defined primarily according to territory, as in the case of neighbourhoods, but even in such cases, proximity or shared territory cannot by itself constitute a community; the relational dimension is also essential.

8.4. Local Community

Local community is a geographically defined community, a group of people living close to each other. The term community suggest that its members have some relations that are communal - experiences, values, and/or interests may be shared, they may interact with each other and are concerned about mutual and collective well-being.

Local community has been an issue of concern in social criticism and theoretical sociology, among others, especially in contrast to the modern society. The central idea, either expressed or rejected, is that local community has been in decline, if not lost, in our contemporary life.

8.4.1. Benefits of Local Community

The benefit of local community is not limited to its appeal to popular imagination. Some empirical and theoretical research has indicated a range of benefits. The interpersonal ties within a local area enables various resource-sharing among the networked people. Lending small amount of money among the individuals is one form of this sharing.

It may take a more subtle form of paying attention to each other and watch delinquent of criminal activities, as well as accident, leading to a higher public safety and lower crime rate.

8.5. Conclusion

Diffusion of innovations research suggests that peer networks play a great role in the process of diffusion of knowledge and practices throughout a society. Medical practices and advice which enhance public health and sanitation would be shared among people more effectively given strong interpersonal networks. Adoption of new technologies would often occur through the network.

References

Aitken, Stuart C., "Public participation, technological discourses and the scale of GIS". In W. Craig, T. Harris, and D. Weiner, eds., *Community Participation and Geographic Information Systems*. Taylor and Francis, 2001.

Aitken, Stuart C.,"Families, communities, and scale of difference", *Social and Cultural Geography* 1(1), 2000.

Jackson, P., "The cultural politics of masculinity: Towards a social geography", *Transactions, Institute of British Geographers,* 1991.

Jordan Terry G. and Lester Rowntree, *The Human Mosaic: A Thematic Introduction to Cultural Geography*, 4th ed., 1986.

Jumper, S.R., "Baccalaureate curricula in geography: Need for consensus guidelines", *Journal of Geography*, 1994.

Knox, Paul, *Urban Social Geography: An Introduction*, 2nd ed., 1987.

Leighly John (ed.), *Land and Life: A Selection from the Writings of Carl Ortwin Sauer*, 1963.

Larkin, Robert P. and Peters, Gary L., *Dictionary of concepts in human geography*, Westport, CT: Greenwood Press, 1983.

Ley, David, *A Social Geography of the City*, 1983.

Marriott, Alan and Sanchez, John, "The integration of family planning and development activities in India", *Geography*, 1998.

Monkhouse, Francis John, *A dictionary of geography*, 2nd ed. London: Edward Arnold, 1970.

Pattison, W.D., "The Four Traditions of Geography", *Journal of Geography*, 1990.

Spencer J.E. and William L. Thomas, *Introducing Cultural Geography*, 2nd ed., 1978.

Thomas William L. (ed.), *Man's Role in Changing the Face of the Earth*, 1956, reissued in 2 vol., 1970.

Wagner Philip L. and Marvin W. Mikesell (eds.), *Readings in Cultural Geography*, 1962.

9

Urban Geography

Urban geography is the study of urban areas, which have a high concentration of buildings and infrastructure. These are areas where the majority of economic activities are in the secondary sector and tertiary sectors. They probably have a high population density. It can be considered a part of the larger field of human geography. However, it can often overlap with other fields such as anthropology and sociology. Urban geographers seek to understand how factors interact over space, what function they serve and their interrelationships.

Urban geographers also look at the development of settlements. Therefore, it involves planning city expansion and improvements. Urban geography, then, attempts to account for the human and environmental impacts of the change. Urban geography forms the theoretical basis for a number of professions including urban planning, retail store site selection, real estate development, crime pattern analysis and logistical analysis.

There are essentially two approaches to urban geography. The study of problems relating to the spatial distribution of cities themselves and the complex patterns of movement, flows and linkages that bind them in space. Studies in this category are concerned with the city system. Secondly there is the study of patterns of distribution and interaction within cities, essentially the study of their inner structure. Studies in this category are concerned with the city as a system.

9.1. Site and Situation

Site describes the location of a city with respect to its soil, water supply and relief, or more still the actual point on which a settlement is built while situation describes the surrounds of the city in terms of other settlements, rivers, mountains and communication. Locations for cities are usually chosen for good reasons. Benefits of certain locations can include:

— *A wet area*: water is a constant necessity for urban areas and is difficult to transport. For this reason many cities are located near or adjacent to rivers.

— *A dry area*: in wet areas a dry area offers protection from flooding and marshland.

— *Easy access to building materials*: stone, wood or clay are necessary for the construction of cities and are difficult to transport long distances.

— *A strategic defensive position*: historically many cities have been constructed on high ground in order to make attack more difficult and to give a good view of surrounding land. River meanders are also used as partial moats.

— *Fuel supply*: most cities were initially constructed near wood for burning and cooking. Today many cities are constructed near coal, oil and gas mines to make use of those resources.

— *A food supply*: cities need some nearby land to be suitable for animal grazing or crop growing

— *A travel intersection point and bridging points*: it is often useful for a city to be located at the intersection of rivers, roads or train lines in order to facilitate travel and trade. Bridging points are shallow areas that allow easy construction of bridges.

— *Shelter and aspect*: it is desirable to construct cities located on the side of a slope that is protected from incoming winds, and in a direction that receives maximum sun exposure.

9.2. City System

Much of the world is increasingly urbanised. Before 1850 no country could claim to be predominantly urbanised and at the turn of the century, only Great Britain could be regarded as such.

9.3. URBANISATION

Urbanisation is the process whereby society is transformed from an essentially rural one to a predominantly urban one. Its most visible expression in the landscape is the growth of cities and an increase in their number, size and importance. Also, urbanisation process can be closely allied with economic colonisation.

Urbanisation, however is not just the growth of cities but rather it is a complex change in economic, social and political thinking. As cities grow, new definitions have been introduced for census purposes in which the concept of the "extended city" is commonly used. Definitions such as the urban area based on the physical extent of the built-up area and minimum requirements of population size and density as well as the metropolitan area, based on urban population size and commute patterns as a measure of spatial integration give us a much better indication of the population size of cities than the use of political entities like the municipality. One of the definitions that have raised much interest is that based on the concept of urban field which is a new form of urban habitat of relatively low density involving a good transportation system and a broad array of economic, social and recreational opportunities. Each urban field is centered on and dominated to a certain extent by a metropolitan area of at least 200,000-300,000 people. It's outer limits can be defined by two criteria: (1) The maximum time or distance that most people are prepared to commute. (2) The time or distance that most people are prepared to spend travelling to or from weekly or weekend recreational activities. Many of these urban fields come into contact with each other and they interact cities do not and cannot exist in isolation. In order for the surplus to be concentrated at particular locations linkages were necessary and cities became nodes in networks comprising of the movement of goods, services, materials, people, money, credit, investment and information.

The diffusion of innovations is the ideal example of the function of the urban hierarchy. Large cities are more likely places for invention and innovation to occur and spread or diffuse to other cities below it in the hierarchy. As some cities grew and become more important they climb the hierarchy, with major metropolitan centers at the top and towns, villages and hamlets at the bottom.

9.4. Cities of Manufacturing and Services

Cities differ in their economic makeup, their social and demographic characteristics and the roles they play within the city system. These differences can be traced back to regional variations in the local resources on which growth was based during the early development of the urban pattern and in part the subsequent shifts in the competitive advantage of regions brought about by changing locational forces affecting regional specialisation within the framework of the market economy. Recognition of different city types necessitates their classification, and it is to this important aspect of urban geography that we now turn. Emphasis is on functional town classification and the basic underlying dimensions of the city system.

The purpose of classifying cities is twofold. On the one hand, it is undertaken in order to search reality for hypotheses. In this context, the recognition of different types of cities on the basis of, for example, their functional specialisation may enable the identification of spatial regularities in the distribution and structure of urban functions and the formulation of hypotheses about the resulting patterns. On the other hand, classification is undertaken to structure reality in order to test specific hypotheses that have already been formulated. For example, to test the hypotheses that cities with a diversified economy grow at a faster rate then those with a more specialised economic base, cities must first be classified so that diversified and specialised cities can be differentiated.

The simplest way to classify cities is to identify the distinctive role they play in the city system. There are three distinct roles.

i) Central places functioning primarily as service centers for local hinterlands.

ii) Transportation cities performing break-of-bulk and allied functions for larger regions.

iii) Specialised-function cities are dominated by one activity such as mining, manufacturing or recreation and serving national and international markets.

The composition of a cities labour force has traditionally been regarded as the best indicator of functional specialisation, and different city types have been most frequently indentified from the analysis of employment profiles. Specialisation in a given activity is said to exist when employment in it exceeds some critical level.

The relationship between the city system and the development of manufacturing has become very apparent. The rapid growth and spread of cities within the heartland-hinterland frameworkafter 1870 was conditioned to a large extent by industrial developments and that the decentralisation of population within the urban system in recent years is related in large part to the movement of employment in manufacturing away from the traditional industrial centers. Manufacturing is found in nearly all cities, but its importance is measured by the proportion of total earnings received by the inhabitants of an urban area. When 25 percent or more of the total earnings in an urban region are derived from manufacturing, that urban areas is arbitrarily designated as a manufacturing center.

The location of manufacturing is affected by myriad economic and non-economic factors, such as the nature of the material inputs, the factors of production, the market and transportation costs. Other important influences include agglomeration and external economies, public policy and personal preferences. Although it is difficult to evaluate precisely the effect of the market on the location of manufacturing activities, two considerations are involved: the nature of and demand for the product and transportation costs.

9.5. Urban Area

An urban area is an area with an increased density of human-created structures in comparison to the areas surrounding it. This term is at one end of the spectrum of suburban and rural areas. An urban area is more frequently called a city or town. Urban areas are created and further developed by the process of urbanisation. Measuring the extent of an urbanised area helps in analysing population density and urban sprawl, and in determining urban and rural populations.

Unlike an urban area, a metropolitan area includes not only the urban area, but also satellite cities plus intervening rural land that is socio-economically connected to the urban core city, typically by employment ties through commuting, with the urban core city being the primary labour market. This makes metropolitan areas a less relevant statistic for determining per capita land usage and densities.

The minimum density requirement is generally 400 persons per square kilometre. In Australia, urban areas are referred to as "urban centres" and are defined as population clusters of 1000 or more people, with a minimum density of 200 people per square kilometre. In Japan urbanised areas are defined as contiguous areas of densely inhabited districts (DIDs) using census enumeration districts as units with a density requirement of 4,000 people per square kilometre.

European countries define urbanised areas on the basis of urban-type land use, not allowing any gaps of typically more than 200 meters, and use satellite photos instead of census blocks to determine the boundaries of the urban area. In less developed countries, in addition to land use and density requirements, a requirement that a large majority of the population, typically 75%, is not engaged in agriculture and/or fishing is sometimes used. Statistics New Zealand defines New Zealand urban areas for statistical purposes as a settlement with a population of a thousand people or more.

In Canada, an urban area is an area that has more than 400 people per square kilometre and has more than 1,000 people. If two or more urban areas are within two kilometres of each other, they are merged into a single urban area. The boundaries of an urban area are not influenced by municipal or even provincial boundaries.

In France, an urban area is a zone encompassing an area of built-up growth and its commuter belt. Although the official INSEE translation of aire urbaine is "urban area", most North Americans would find the same as being similar in definition to their metropolitan area.

In the United States there are two categories of urban area. The term urbanised area denotes an urban area of 50,000 or more people. Urban areas under 50,000 people are called urban clusters. Urbanised areas were first delineated in the United States in the 1950 census, while urban clusters were added in the 2000 census. There are 1371 United States Urban Areas & Urban Clusters with more than 10,000 people.

The US Census Bureau defines an urban area as: "Core census block groups or blocks that have a population density of at least 1,000 people per square mile (386 per square kilometre) and surrounding census blocks that have an overall density of at least 500 people per square mile (193 per square kilometre)."

The concept of Urbanised Areas as defined by the US Census Bureau are often used as a more accurate gauge of the size of a city, since in different cities and states the lines between city borders and the urbanised area of that city are often not the same. For example, the city of Greenville, South Carolina has a city population under 60,000 but an urbanised area over 300,000, while Greensboro, North Carolina has a city population over 200,000 but an urbanised area population of around 270,000--meaning that Greenville is actually "larger" for some intents and purposes, but not for others, such as taxation, local elections, etc.

9.6. Population Density

Population density is a measurement of population per unit area or unit volume. It is frequently applied to living organisms, humans in particular.

9.6.1. Biological Population Densities

Population density is a common biological measurement and is often used by conservationists and sociobiologists as a more appropriate measure than population size. Low densities may cause an extinction vortex and lead to further reduced fertility. This is called the Allee effect, after W. C. Allee who first identified it. Examples of the causes in low population densities include:

— Increased problems with locating mates

— Increased inbreeding

— Increased susceptibility to catastrophic events

Different species have different expected densities. R-selected species commonly have high population densities, while K-selected species may have lower densities.

Low densities may be associated with specialised mate location adaptations such as specialised pollinators; as found in the orchid family. For humans, population density is the number of persons per unit of area (which may include or exclude cultivated or potentially productive area). Commonly this may be calculated for a county, city, country, another territory, or the entire world.

The world population is 6.5 billion humans, and Earth's area is 510 million square kilometres (200 million square miles). Therefore the world-wide human population density is 6.5 billion / 510 million = 13 per km^2 (33 per sq mi), or 43 per km^2 (112 per sq mi) considering that humans live on land, which forms 150 million km^2 (58 million sq mi) of the earth. This density rises with the population growth.

Several of the highest-density territories in the world are very large city-states, micronations or dependencies. These territories share a relatively small area and an exceptionally high urbanisation level, with an economically specialised city population drawing also on rural resources outside the area, illustrating the difference between high population density and overpopulation.

Cities with exceptionally high population densities are often considered to be overpopulated, though the extent to which this is the case depends on factors like quality of housing and infrastructure or access to resources. City population is however, heavily dependent on the definition used for the urban area: densities will be far higher for the central municipality than when more recently-developed and as yet administratively unincorporated suburbs are included, as in the concepts of agglomeration or metropolitan area, the latter including sometimes neighbouring cities.

9.7. Methods of Measurement

While the arithmetic density is the most common way of measuring population density, several other methods have been developed which aim to provide a more accurate measure of population density over a specific area.

9.7.1. Secondary Sector of Economic Activity

The secondary sector of industry includes those economic sectors that create a finished, usable product: manufacturing and construction. This sector of industry generally takes the output of the primary sector and manufactures finished goods or products to a point where they are suitable for use by other businesses, for export, or sale to domestic consumers. This sector is often divided into light industry and heavy industry. Many of these industries consume large quantities of energy and require factories and machinery to convert the raw materials into goods and products. They also produce waste materials and waste heat that may pose environmental problems or cause pollution.

Some economists contrast wealth producing sectors in an economy such as manufacturing with the service sector which tends to be wealth consuming. Examples of service may include retail, insurance, and government. These economists contend that an economy begins to decline as its wealth producing sector shrinks. Manufacturing is an important activity to promote economic growth and development. Nations which export manufactured products tend to generate higher marginal GDP growth which supports higher incomes and marginal tax revenue needed to fund the quality of life initiatives such as health care and infrastructure in the economy. The field is an important source for engineering job opportunities. Among developed countries, it is an important source of good paying jobs for the middle-class to facilitate greater social mobility for successive generations in an economy.

9.7.2. Tertiary Sector of Economic Activity

The tertiary sector of industry is one of the three main industrial categories of a developed economy, the others being the secondary industry (manufacturing), and primary industry (extraction such as mining, agriculture and fishing). Services are defined in conventional economic literature as "intangible goods".

The tertiary sector of industry involves the provision of services to businesses as well as final consumers. Services may involve the transport, distribution and sale of goods from producer to a consumer as may happen in wholesaling and retailing, or may involve the provision of a service, such as in pest control or entertainment. Goods may be transformed in the process of providing a service, as happens in the restaurant industry or in equipment repair. However, the focus is on people interacting with people and serving the customer rather than transforming physical goods.

9.7.3. Components of Service Sector

The service sector consists of the "soft" parts of the economy such as insurance, government, tourism, banking, retail, education, and social services. In soft-sector employment, people use time to deploy knowledge assets, collaboration assets, and process-engagement to create productivity (effectiveness), performance improvement potential (potential) and sustainability. Typically the output of this time is content (information), service, attention, advice, experiences, and/or discussion (also known as "intangible goods").

Public utilities are often considered part of the tertiary sector as they provide services to people, while creating the utility's infrastructure is often considered part of the secondary sector, even though the same business may be involved in both aspects of the operation.

To do fact-based work in this area it is necessary to utilise the exetensive data collection that takes place using classification systems such as the United Nations's International Standard Industrial Classification standard, the United States' Standard Industrial Classification (SIC) code system and its new replacement, the North American Industrial Classification System (NAICS), and similar systems in the EU and elsewhere.

Since the 1960s, there has been a substantial shift from the other two industry sectors to the Tertiary Sector in industrialised countries. The term service economy, in contrast, refers to a model wherein as much economic activity as possible is treated as a service. For example IBM treats its business as a service business. Although it still manufactures high-end computers, it sees the physical goods as a small part of the "business solutions" industry. They have found that the price elasticity of demand for "business solutions" is much less than that for hardware. There has been a corresponding shift to a subscription pricing model. Rather than receiving a single payment for a piece of manufactured equipment, many manufacturers are now receiving a steady stream of revenue for ongoing contracts.

9.7.4. Theory of Progression

Economies tend to follow a developmental progression that takes them from a heavy reliance on agriculture and mining, toward the development of industry (e.g. automobiles, textiles, shipbuilding, steel) and finally toward a more service based structure. Whereas the first economy to follow this path in the modern world was the United Kingdom, the speed at which other economies have later made the transition to service-based, sometimes called post-industrial, has accelerated over time.

Historically manufacturing tended to be more open to international trade and competition than services. As a result, there has been a tendency for the first economies to industrialise to come under competitive attack by those seeking to industrialise later, e.g. because production, especially labour, costs are lower in those industrialising later. The resultant shrinkage of manufacturing in the leading economies might explain their growing reliance on the service sector.

However, currently and prospectively, with dramatic cost reduction and speed and reliability improvements in the transportation of people and the communication of information, the service sector now includes some of the most intensive international competition, despite residual protectionism.

According to some economists, the service sector tends to be wealth consuming, whereas manufacturing is wealth producing. Sir Keith Joseph in his lecture Monetarism IS Not Enough, contrasted wealth-producing sectors in an economy such as manufacturing with the service sector which tends to be a wealth-consuming sector. He contended that an economy declines as its wealth-producing sector begins to shrink.

Service providers face obstacles selling services that goods-sellers rarely face. Services are not tangible, making it difficult for potential customers to understand what they will receive and what value it will hold for them. Indeed some, such as consulting and investment services, offer no guarantees of the value for price paid.

Since the quality of most services depends largely on the quality of the individuals providing the services, it is true that "people costs" are a high component of service costs. Whereas a manufacturer may use technology, simplification, and other techniques to lower the cost of goods sold, the service provider often faces an unrelenting pattern of increasing costs.

9.8. Conclusion

The various forms of flows, movements, transactions and linkages are collectively referred to as spatial interaction and acts as the key to the city system. Interaction then plays a number of crucial roles in shaping the form and structure of city systems, as it does in the internal structure of cities. Four roles the city system plays are particularly important. Firstly, in the same way that the market economy is integrated through price-fixing mechanisms, so interaction performs a spatial integrating role. Second, interaction permits differentiation of functional specialisation of cities within the city system. Third and most important, interaction is the medium of spatial organisation. Lastly, interaction is extremely important in bringing about change and the reorganisation of spatial relationships within the city system.

References

Berry, Brian J.L., *Comparative Urbanization*, rev. and enl. 2nd ed., 1981.

Bourne L.S., R. Sinclair, and K. Dziewónski (eds.), *Urbanization and Settlement Systems*, 1984.

Harold Carter, *The Study of Urban Geography*, 3rd ed., 1981.

Herbert David T. and Colin J. Thomas, *Urban Geography*, 1982.

Jean Gottmann, *Megalopolis: The Urbanized Northeastern Seaboard of the United States*, 1961.

Maurice Yeates and Barry Garner, *The North American City*, 3rd ed., 1980.

Risa Palm, *The Geography of American Cities*, 1981.

Stanley D. Brunn and Jack F. Williams (eds.), *Cities of the World: World Regional Urban Development*, 1983.

______________ and James O. Wheeler (eds.), *The American Metropolitan System*, 1980.

Truman Asa Hartshorn, *Interpreting the City: An Urban Geography*, 1980.

10

Health Geography

Health geography is the application of geographical information, perspectives, and methods to the study of health, disease, and health care. Health is the level of functional and/or metabolic efficiency of an organism at both the micro (cellular) and macro (social) level. In the medical field, health is commonly defined as an organism's ability to efficiently respond to challenges (stressors) and effectively restore and sustain a "state of balance", known as homeostasis.

Another widely accepted definition of health is that of the World Health Organisation (WHO), which states that "health is a state of complete physical, mental and social well-being and not merely the absence of disease or infirmity". In more recent years, this statement has been modified to include the ability to lead a "socially and economically productive life." The WHO definition is not without criticism, as some argue that health cannot be defined as a state at all, but must be seen as a process of continuous adjustment to the changing demands of living and of the changing meanings we give to life. The WHO definition is therefore considered by many as an idealistic goal rather than a realistic proposition.

10.1. Determinants of Health

The LaLonde report suggested that there are four general determinants of health including human biology, environment, lifestyle, and healthcare services. Thus, health is maintained and improved not only through the advancement and application of health science, but also through the efforts and intelligent lifestyle choices of the individual.

Exercising and eating a healthy diet to reduce body fat and attain physical fitness, managing stress, and stopping smoking and other substance abuse are examples of ways to improve one's health. An increasing measure of the health of populations is height, which is strongly influenced by nutrition and health care, and by standard of living and quality of life matters. The study of human growth, its regulators, and its implications is known as auxology.

10.1.1. Wellness

Wellness is a term sometimes used to describe the psychological state of being healthy, but is most often used in the field of alternative medicine to describe one's state of being. This term however is quite hard to fully define.

Workplace wellness programmes are recognised by an increasingly large number of companies for their value in improving health and well-being of their employees, and for increasing morale, loyalty, and productivity. Workplace wellness programmes can include things like onsite fitness centers, health presentations, wellness newsletters, access to health coaching, tobacco cessation programmes and training related to nutrition, weight and stress management. Other programmes may include health risk assessments, health screenings and body mass index monitoring. Mostly overseen or not mentioned is a group of determinants of health which could be called coincidence, hazard, luck or bad luck. These factors are quite important determinants of health but difficult to calculate.

10.1.2. Health Science

Health science is the branch of science dealing with health, and it includes many subdisciplines. There are two approaches to health science: the study and research of the human body and health-related issues to understand how humans (and animals) function, and the application of that knowledge to improve health and to prevent and cure diseases.

Health research builds primarily on the basic sciences of biology, chemistry, and physics as well as a variety of multidisciplinary fields (for example medical sociology). Some of the other primarily research-oriented fields that make exceptionally significant contributions to health science are biochemistry, epidemiology, and genetics.

Applied health sciences also endeavour to better understand health, but in addition they try to directly improve it. Some of these are: biomedical engineering, biotechnology, nursing, nutrition, pharmacology, pharmacy, public health, psychology, physical therapy, and medicine. The provision of services to improve people's health is referred to as health care.

10.1.3. Health Care

Health care is the prevention, treatment, and management of illness and the preservation of mental and physical well being through the services offered by the medical, nursing, and allied health professions. According to the World Health Organisation, health care embraces all the goods and services designed to promote health, including "preventive, curative and palliative interventions, whether directed to individuals or to populations". The organised provision of such services may constitute a health care system. This can include a specific governmental organisation such as the National Health Service in the UK, or a cooperation across the National Health Service and Social Services as in Shared Care.

10.1.4. Physical Exercise

A U.S. Marine emerges from the water upon completing the swimming leg of a triathlon. Exercise is the performance of some activity in order to develop or maintain physical fitness and overall health. It is often directed toward also honing athletic ability or skill. Frequent and regular physical exercise is an important component in the prevention of some of the diseases of affluence such as cancer, heart disease, cardiovascular disease, Type 2 diabetes, obesity and back pain.

Physical exercise is considered important for maintaining physical fitness including healthy weight; building and maintaining healthy bones, muscles, and joints; promoting physiological well-being; reducing surgical risks; and strengthening the immune system. Proper nutrition is just as, if not more, important to health as exercise. When exercising it becomes even more important to have good diet to ensure the body has the correct ratio of macronutrients whilst providing ample micronutrients; this is to aid the body with the recovery process following strenuous exercise. When the body falls short of proper nutrition, it gets into starvation mode developed through evolution and depends onto fat content for survival. Research suggest that the production of thyroid hormones can be negatively affected by repeated bouts of dieting and calorie restriction. Proper rest and recovery is also as important to health as exercise, otherwise the body exists in a permanently injured state and will not improve or adapt adequately to the exercise.

The above two factors can be compromised by psychological compulsions (eating disorders such as exercise bulimia, anorexia, and other bulimias), misinformation, a lack of organisation, or a lack of motivation. These all lead to a decreased state of health. Delayed Onset Muscle Soreness can occur after any exercise, particularly if the body is in an unconditioned state relative to that exercise.

10.1.5. Nutrition

The updated USDA food pyramid, published in 2005, is a general nutrition guide for recommended food consumption. Nutrition is a science which studies the relationship between diet and states of health and disease. Dietitians are Health professionals who are specialised in this area of expertise. They are also the only highly trained health professionals able to provide safe, evidence-based and accurate dietary advice and interventions.

Between extremes of optimal health and death from starvation or malnutrition, there is an array of disease states that can be caused or alleviated by changes in diet. Deficiencies, excesses and imbalances in diet can produce negative impacts on health, which may lead to diseases such as scurvy, obesity or osteoporosis, as well as psychological and behavioural problems. Moreover, excessive ingestion of elements that have no apparent role in health, (e.g. lead, mercury, PCBs, dioxins), may incur toxic and potentially lethal effects, depending on the dose. The science of nutrition attempts to understand how and why specific dietary aspects influence health.

10.1.6. Mental Health

Mental health is a concept that refers to a human individual's emotional and psychological well-being. It is a state of emotional and psychological well-being in which an individual is able to use his or her cognitive and emotional capabilities, function in society, and meet the ordinary demands of everyday life. Cultural differences, subjective assessments, and competing professional theories all affect how "mental health" is defined. In general, "mental health" and "mental illness" are not opposites. In other words, the absence of a recognised mental disorder is not necessarily an indicator of mental health.

One way to think about mental health is by looking at how effectively and successfully a person functions. Feeling capable and competent; being able to handle normal levels of stress, maintain satisfying relationships, and lead an independent life; and being able to "bounce back," or recover from difficult situations, are all signs of mental health.

Encompassing your emotional, social, and-most importantly-your mental well-being; All these aspects-emotional, physical, and social-must function together to achieve overall health.

10.1.7. Disease

A disease is an abnormal condition of an organism that impairs bodily functions. In human beings, "disease" is often used more broadly to refer to any condition that causes discomfort, dysfunction, distress, social problems, and/or death to the person afflicted, or similar problems for those in contact with the person. In this broader sense, it sometimes includes injuries, disabilities, disorders, syndromes, infections, isolated symptoms, deviant behaviours, and atypical variations of structure and function, while in other contexts and for other purposes these may be considered distinguishable categories.

While many diseases are biological processes with observable alterations of organ function or structure, others primarily involve alterations of behaviour.

Classifying a condition as a disease is a social act of valuation, and may change the social status of the person with the condition (the patient). Some conditions (known as culture-bound syndromes) are only recognised as diseases within a particular culture. Sometimes the categorisaton of a condition as a disease is controversial within the culture.

10.1.7.1. Causes of disease

Many different factors intrinsic or extrinsic to a person (or plant or animal) can cause disease. Examples of intrinsic factors are genetic defects or nutritional deficiencies. An environmental exposure, such as second-hand smoke is an example of an extrinsic factor. Many diseases result from a combination of intrinsic and extrinsic factors. For many diseases a cause cannot be identified.

There are many different factors that can cause disease. These can be broadly categorised into the following categories like social, psychological, chemical and biological. Some factors may fall into more than one category. Biochemical causes of disease can be considered as a spectrum where at one extreme disease is caused entirely by genetic factors and at the other extreme is caused entirely by environmental factors. Environmental factors include toxic chemicals and infectious agents. Absence of the genetic or environmental factors in this case results in disease not being manifest. Koch's postulates can be used to determine whether a disease is caused by an infectious agent.

To determine whether a disease is caused by genetic factors, researchers study the pattern inheritance of the disease in families. This provides qualitative information about the disease. To determine to what extent a disease is caused by genetic factors (quantitative information), twin studies are used. Monozygotic twins are genetically identical and likely share a similar environment whereas dizygotic twins are genetically similar and likely share a similar environment. Thus by comparing the incidence of disease (termed concordance rate) in monozygotic twins with the incidence of disease in dizygotic twins, the extent to which genes contribute to disease can be determined. Candidate disease genes can be identified using a number of methods. One is to look for mutants of a model organism that have a similar phenotype to the disease being studied.

The terms disease, disorder, medical condition are often used interchangeably. There is no agreed-upon universal distinction between these terms, though some people do make distinctions in particular contexts.

Medical usage sometimes distinguishes a disease, which has a known specific cause or causes (called its etiology), from a syndrome, which is a collection of signs or symptoms that occur together. However, many conditions have been identified, yet continue to be referred to as "syndromes." Furthermore, numerous conditions of unknown etiology are referred to as "diseases" in many contexts. Refractory diseases do not respond to therapy by overcoming the resistance to drugs.

Illness, although often used to mean disease, can also refer to a person's perception of their health, regardless of whether they in fact have a disease. A person without any disease may feel unhealthy and simply have the perception of having an illness. Another person may feel healthy with similar perceptions of perfectly good health. The individual's perception of good health may even persist with the medical diagnosis of having a disease; for example, such as dangerously high blood pressure, which may lead to a fatal heart attack or stroke.

Pathology is the study of diseases. The subject of systematic classification of diseases is referred to as nosology. Its cause is referred as its etiology. The broader body of knowledge about human diseases and their treatments is medicine. Many similar (and a few of the same) conditions or processes can affect non-human animals (wild or domestic). The study of diseases affecting animals is veterinary medicine.

Disease can be thought of as the presence of pathology, which can occur with or without subjective feelings of being unwell or social recognition of that state. Illness as the subjective state of "unwellness" can occur independently of, or in conjunction with, disease or sickness, which can also occur independently of the presence or absence of disease or illness. Thus, someone with undetected high blood pressure who feels to be of good health would be diseased, but not ill or sick. Someone with a diagnosis of late-stage cancer would be diseased, probably feeling quite ill, and recognised by others as sick. A person incarcerated in a totalitarian psychiatric hospital for political purposes could arguably be then said to not be diseased, nor ill, but only classified as sick by the rulers of a society with which the person did not agree. Having had a bad day after a night of excess drinking, one might feel ill, but one would not be diseased, nor is it likely that a boss could be convinced of the sickness.

10.1.7.2. Transmission of disease

Some diseases such as influenza are contagious or infectious. Infectious diseases can be transmitted by any of a variety of mechanisms, including aerosols produced by coughs and sneezes, by bites of insects or other carriers of the disease, and from contaminated water or food (possibly by faeces or urine in the sewage), etc. When micro-organisms that cannot be spread from person to person might play a role, some diseases can be prevented with proper nutrition. Other diseases such as cancer and heart disease are not considered to be caused by infection. The same is true of mental diseases.

10.1.7.3. Social significance of disease

Living with disease can be very difficult. The identification of a condition as a disease, rather than as simply a variation of human structure or function, can have significant social or economic implications. The controversial recognitions as diseases of post-traumatic stress disorder, also known as "Soldier's heart," "shell shock," and "combat fatigue;" repetitive motion injury or repetitive stress injury (RSI); and Gulf War syndrome has had a number of positive and negative effects on the financial and other responsibilities of governments, corporations and institutions towards individuals, as well as on the individuals themselves. The social implication of viewing aging as a disease could be profound, though this classification is not yet widespread.

A condition may be considered to be a disease in some cultures or eras but not in others. Oppositional-defiant disorder, attention-deficit hyperactivity disorder, and, increasingly, obesity, are conditions considered to be diseases in the United States and Canada today, but were not so-considered decades ago and are not so-considered in some other countries. Lepers were a group of afflicted individuals who were historically shunned and the term "leper" still evokes social stigma. Fear of disease can still be a widespread social phenomena, though not all diseases evoke extreme social stigma.

Sickness confers the social legitimisation of certain benefits, such as illness benefits, work avoidance, and being looked after by others. In return, there is an obligation on the sick person to seek treatment and work to become well once more. As a comparison, consider pregnancy, which is not a state interpreted as disease or sickness by the individual. On the other hand, it is considered by the medical community as a condition requiring medical care and by society at large as a condition requiring one's staying at home from work.

10.1.7.4. Global disease burden

Health care, or healthcare, is the prevention, treatment, and management of illness and the preservation of mental and physical well being through the services offered by the medical, nursing, and allied health professions. According to the World Health Organisation, health care embraces all the goods and services designed to promote health, including "preventive, curative and palliative interventions, whether directed to individuals or to populations". The organised provision of such services may constitute a health care system. This can include a specific governmental organisation such as, in the UK, the National Health Service or a cooperation across the National Health Service and Social Services as in Shared Care. Before the term "health care" became popular, English-speakers referred to medicine or to the health sector and spoke of the treatment and prevention of illness and disease. In most developed countries and many developing countries health care is provided to everyone regardless of their ability to pay.

10.1.8. Health Care Industry

The health care industry is considered an industry or profession which includes peoples exercise of skill or judgment or the providing of a service related to the preservation or improvement of the health of individuals or the treatment or care of individuals who are injured, sick, disabled, or infirm. The delivery of modern health care depends on an expanding group of trained professionals coming together as an interdisciplinary team.

The health care industry is one of the world's largest and fastest-growing industries. Consuming over 10 percent of gross domestic product of most developed nations, health care can form an enormous part of a country's economy. In 2003, health care costs paid to hospitals, physicians, nursing homes, diagnostic laboratories, pharmacies, medical device manufacturers and other components of the health care system, consumed 15.3 percent of the GDP of the United States, the largest of any country in the world.

10.1.9. Health Care Systems

Purely private enterprise health care systems are comparatively rare. Where they exist, it is usually for a comparatively well-off sub-population in a poorer country with a poorer standard of health care-for instance, private clinics for a small, wealthy expatriate population in an otherwise poor country. But there are countries with a majority-private health care system with residual public service. The other major models are public insurance systems. A Social security health care model is where workers and their families are insured by the State. A Publicly funded health care model is where the residents of the country are insured by the State. Within this branch is Single-payer health care, which describes a type of financing system in which a single entity, typically a government run organisation, acts as the administrator (or "payer") to collect all health care fees, and pay out all health care costs.

Some advocates of universal health care assert that single-payer systems save money that could be used directly towards health care by reducing administrative waste. In practice this means that the government collects taxes from the public, businesses, etc., creates an entity to administer the supply of health care and then pays health care professionals. Harry Wachtel estimate a single payer universal healthcare system will actually save money through reduced bureaucratic administration costs. Social health insurance is where the whole population or most of the population is a member of a sickness insurance company. Most health services are provided by private enterprises which act as contractors, billing the government for patient care. In almost every country with a government health care system a parallel private system is allowed to operate. This is sometimes referred to as two-tier health care. The scale, extent, and funding of these private systems is very variable.

A traditional view is that improvements in health result from advancements in medical science. The medical model of health focuses on the eradication of illness through diagnosis and effective treatment. In contrast, the social model of health places emphasis on changes that can be made in society and in people's own lifestyles to make the population healthier. It defines illness from the point of view of the individual's functioning within their society rather than by monitoring for changes in biological or physiological signs.

10.2. World Health Organisation

The World Health Organisation (WHO) is a specialised United Nations agency which acts as a coordinator and researcher for public health around the world. Established on April 1948, and headquartered in Geneva, Switzerland, the agency inherited the mandate and resources of its predecessor, the Health Organisation, which had been an agency of the League of Nations. The WHO's constitution states that its mission "is the attainment by all peoples of the highest possible level of health." Its major task is to combat disease, especially key infectious diseases, and to promote the general health of the peoples of the world. Examples of its work include years of fighting smallpox. In 1979 the WHO declared that the disease had been eradicated - the first disease in history to be completely eliminated by deliberate human design. The WHO is nearing success in developing vaccines against malaria and schistosomiasis and aims to eradicate polio within the next few years. The organisation has already endorsed the world's first official HIV/AIDS Toolkit for Zimbabwe from October 3, 2006, making it an international standard.

The WHO is financed by contributions from member states and from donors. In recent years the WHO's work has involved more collaboration, currently around 80 such partnerships, with NGOs and the pharmaceutical industry, as well as with foundations such as the Bill and Melinda Gates Foundation and the Rockefeller Foundation. Voluntary contributions to the WHO from national and local governments, foundations and NGOs, other UN organisations, and the private sector (including pharmaceutical companies), now exceed that of assessed contributions (dues) from its 193 member nations.

Australia and New Zealand both have publicly funded health care systems, though under the Conservative government in Australia, there has been new funding and incentives for people who pay for private health insurance.

Medicare was introduced by the Whitlam Labour Government on 1 July 1975 through the Health Insurance Act 1973. The Australian Senate rejected the changes multiple times and they were passed only after a joint sitting after the 1974 double dissolution election. Yet Medicare has been supported by subsequent governments and became a key feature of Australia's public policy landscape. The exact structure of Medicare, in terms of the size of the rebate to doctors and hospitals and the way it has administered, has varied over the years. The original Medicare programme proposed a 1.35% levy (with low income exemptions) but these bills were rejected by the Senate, and so Medicare was originally funded from general taxation.

All of Europe has publicly sponsored and regulated health care. Countries include Austria, Belgium, Denmark, Finland, France, Germany, Greece, Hungary, Ireland, Italy, Slovenia, the Netherlands, Norway, Poland, Portugal, Romania, Russia, Spain, Sweden and the United Kingdom.

The Health Insurance Institute of Slovenia (the Institute) was founded on March 1, 1992, according to the Law on health care and health insurance, after declaring independence from Yugoslavia. The Institute conducts its business as a public institute, bound by statute to provide compulsory health insurance. In the field of compulsory health insurance, the Institute's principal task is to provide effective collection (mobilisation) and distribution (allocation) of public funds, in order to ensure the insured persons quality rights arising from the said funds. The rights arising from compulsory health insurance, furnished by the funds collected by means of compulsory insurance contributions, comprise the rights to health care services and rights to several financial benefits (sick leave pay, reimbursement of travel costs and funeral costs, and insurance money paid in case of death).

Healthcare in Switzerland is regulated by the Federal Health Insurance Act. Health insurance is compulsory for all persons resident in Switzerland. International civil servants, members of permanent missions and their family members are exempted from compulsory health insurance. They can, however, apply to join the Swiss health insurance system, within six months of taking up residence in the country. Health insurance covers the costs of medical treatment and hospitalisation of the insured.

The logo of the NHS in England. The colour, "NHS Blue," is used on signs and leaflets throughout the English NHS. The NHS is the world's largest, centralised health service, and the world's third largest employer after the Chinese army and the Indian railways. The first PFI hospitals contain some 28 per cent fewer beds than the ones they replaced. Even so there is for the first time complete political consensus on the importance of free public health care.

Most countries in Latin America have public health care provided. Mexico is planning to launch its own universal health care network though at the moment the standards of health care in Mexico are seriously lacking with large divides between rich and poor. Puerto Rico is planning its own health reform for the poorest of the population. Health care in Venezuela is probably the most extensive and given the country's fortunes in oil wealth, expenditure has recently increased greatly, starting with mass vaccinations under the Plan Bolivar 2000.

The Cuban government operates a national health system and assumes fiscal and administrative responsibility for the health care of its citizens. Beginning in 1960, the Ministry of Public Health began a programme of nationalisation and regionalisation of medical services. In 1976, Cuba's healthcare programme was enshrined in Article 50 of the revised Cuban constitution which states

Like the rest of the Cuban economy, Cuban medical care has suffered from severe material shortages following the end of Soviet subsidies and the ongoing United States embargo against Cuba that began after the Cuban Missile Crisis.

The federal government of Lester B. Pearson, pressured by the New Democratic Party (NDP) who held the balance of power, introduced the Medical Care Act in 1966 that extended the HIDS Act cost-sharing to allow each province to establish a universal health care plan. It also set up the Medicare system. In 1984, the Canada Health Act was passed, which prohibited user fees and extra billing by doctors. The Canadian system is for the most part publicly funded, yet most of the services are provided by private enterprises, private corporations. Most all doctors do not receive an annual salary, but receive a fee per visit or service. This mostly goes towards services not covered or only partially covered by Medicare such as prescription drugs, dentistry and optometry. Many Canadians have private health insurance, often through their employers, that cover these expenses.

In the United States, certain publicly funded health care programmes help to provide for the elderly, disabled, military service families and veterans, children, and the poor, and federal law ensures public access to emergency services regardless of ability to pay; however, a system of universal health care has not been implemented. The Commonwealth of Massachusetts is attempting to implement a near-universal health care system by mandating that residents purchase health insurance by July 1, 2007. California, Maine, Pennsylvania, and Vermont also are attempting universal systems at the state level, with some smaller locations such as San Francisco also attempting this at the citywide level. Some government health care systems allow private practitioners to provide services, and some do not.

Health care in India is guaranteed to "improve" for all under the constitution, although the reality does not live up to the vague wording of the article. In Sri Lanka, drugs are provided by a government owned drug manufacturer called the State Pharmaceuticals Corporation of Sri Lanka. In the Philippines, the Department of Health (Philippines) organises public health for the country, and was established at the initiative of the American governors, before independence. Saudi Arabia has a publicly funded health system, although its levels are lower than the regional average.

In Japan, payment for personal medical services is offered through a universal insurance system that provides relative equality of access, with fees set by a government committee. People without insurance through employers can participate in a national health insurance programme administered by local governments. In addition to cost-control problems, the system was troubled with excessive paperwork, long waits to see physicians, assembly-line care for out-patients, over medication, and abuse of the system because of low out-of-pocket costs to patients. Another problem is an uneven distribution of health personnel, with cities favoured over rural areas.

Health care in Africa is usually non existent or highly limited and under resourced. The outbreak and spread of HIV/AIDS in Africa has crippled many populations and sent life expectancies plummeting. However some countries have been able to tackle the challenges, for instance health care in Uganda as well as education has reduced HIV/AIDS infections from 13% to 4.1% from 1990 to 2003. This contrasts to some governments' approach, especially that of the South African Health Ministry who until recently denied the link between HIV/AIDS.

Health care provision in Nigeria is a concurrent responsibility of the three tiers of government in the country. However, because Nigeria operates a mixed economy, private providers of health care have a visible role to play in health care delivery. The federal government's role is mostly limited to coordinating the affairs of the university teaching hospitals, while the state government manages the various general hospitals and the local government focus on dispensaries.

Historically, health insurance in Nigeria can be applied to a few instances: free health care provided and financed for all citizens, health care provided by government through a special health insurance scheme for government employees and private firms entering contracts with private health care providers. However, there are few people who fall within the three instances. In May 1999, the government created the National Health Insurance Scheme, the scheme encompasses government employees, the organised private sector and the informal sector. Legislative wise, the scheme also covers children under five, permanently disabled persons and prison inmates. In 2004, the administration of Obasanjo further gave more legislative powers to the scheme with positive amendments to the original 1999 legislative act.

10.3. Geography of Health Care Provision

Although health care is a public good, it is not 'pure'. In other words, it is not equally available to all individuals. The geography of health care provision has much to do with this. Demand for public services is continuously distributed across space, broadly in accordance with the distribution of population, but these services are only provided at discrete locations. Inevitably therefore, there will be inequalities of access in terms of the practicality of using services, transport costs, travel times and so on. Geographical or 'locational' factors are not the only aspects which influence access to health care. Other types (or dimensions) of accessibility to health care except for geographical (or spatial) are social, financial and functional. Social accessibility to health care depends on race, age, sex and other social characteristics of individuals, important here is also relationship between patient and the doctor. Financial depends upon the price of a particular health care and functional reflects the amount and structure of provided services. This can vary among different countries or regions of the world. Access to health care is influenced also by factors such as opening times and waiting lists that play an important part in determining whether individuals or population sub-groups can access health care - this type of accessibility is termed 'effective accessibility'.

The location of health care facilities depends largely on the nature of the health care system in operation, and will be heavily influenced by historical factors due to the heavy investment costs in facilities such as hospitals and surgeries. Simple distance will be mediated by organisational factors such as the existence of a referral system by which patients are directed towards particular parts of the hospital sector by their GP. Access to primary care is therefore a very significant component of access to the whole system.

10.4. Alternative Medicine

Alternative medicine has been described as "any of various systems of healing or treating disease (as chiropractic, homeopathy, or faith healing) not included in the traditional medical curricula taught in the United States and Britain". Alternative medicine practices are often based in belief systems that are at odds with the findings of science. Alternative medicines may therefore incorporate spiritual, metaphysical, or religious underpinnings, untested practices, non-Western medical traditions, or newly developed approaches to healing.

If an alternative medical approach, initially regarded as untested, is subsequently shown to be safe and effective, it may then be adopted by conventional practitioners and no

Alternative medicine is commonly categorised together with complementary medicine under the umbrella term 'complementary and alternative medicine' (CAM for short). Some scientists reject this and the above classifications and to varying degrees reject the term "alternative medicine" itself.

The following three commentators argue for classifying treatments based on the objectively verifiable criteria of the scientific method, not based on the changing curricula of various medical schools or social sphere of usage. They advocate a classification based on evidence-based medicine, i.e., scientifically proven evidence of efficacy (or lack thereof).

Some commentators maintain that some or all fields of alternative medicine are pseudo-scientific, or contain significant pseudo-scientific elements. In the late 20th century systematic investigation of the evidence-base proceeded, and at least one university department of alternative and complementary medicine was established, at the University of Exeter under Professor Edzard Ernst for this purpose.

Jurisdiction differs concerning which branches of alternative medicine are legal, which are regulated, and which (if any) are provided by a government-controlled health service or reimbursed by a private health medical insurance company. Obligations to respect (the right to health) include a State's obligation to refrain from prohibiting or impeding traditional preventive care, healing practices and medicines, from marketing unsafe drugs and from applying coercive medical treatments

A number of alternative medicine advocates disagree with the restrictions of government agencies that approve medical treatments and the agencies' adherence to experimental evaluation methods. They claim that this impedes those seeking to bring useful and effective treatments and approaches to the public, and protest that their contributions and discoveries are unfairly dismissed, overlooked or suppressed. Alternative medicine providers often argue that health fraud should be dealt with appropriately when it occurs.

In India, which is the home of several alternative systems of medicines, Ayurveda, Siddha, Unani, and Homeopathy are licensed by the government, despite lack of reputable scientific evidence. Naturopathy will also be licensed soon because several Universities now offer bachelors degrees in it. Other activities connected with AM/CM, such as Panchakarma and massage therapy related to Ayurveda are also licensed by the government now. Research into and licensing of these activities is carried out by the Department of Ayurveda, Yoga & Naturopathy, Unani, Siddha and Homoeopathy (AYUSH).

Many people utilise mainstream medicine for diagnosis and basic information, while turning to alternatives for what they believe to be health-enhancing measures. However, studies indicate that the majority of people use alternative approaches in conjunction with conventional medicine.

Alternative therapies provide some services not available from conventional medicine. Examples are patient empowerment and treatment methods that follow the biopsychosocial model of health.

Advocates of alternative medicine hold that the various alternative treatment methods are effective in treating a wide range of major and minor medical conditions, and contend that recently published research proves the effectiveness of specific alternative treatments. Advocates of alternative medicine hold that alternative medicine may provide health benefits through patient empowerment, by offering more choices to the public, including treatments that are simply not available in conventional medicine:

"Most Americans who consult alternative providers would probably jump at the chance to consult a physician who is well trained in scientifically based medicine and who is also open-minded and knowledgeable about the body's innate mechanisms of healing, the role of lifestyle factors in influencing health, and the appropriate uses of dietary supplements, herbs, and other forms of treatment, from osteopathic manipulation to Chinese and Ayurvedic medicine. In other words, they want competent help in navigating the confusing maze of therapeutic options that are available today, especially in those cases in which conventional approaches are relatively ineffective or harmful."

Evidence-based medicine (EBM) applies the scientific method to medical practice, and aims for the ideal that healthcare professionals should make "conscientious, explicit, and judicious use of current best evidence" in their everyday practice.

Although advocates of alternative medicine acknowledge that the placebo effect may play a role in the benefits that some receive from alternative therapies, they point out that this does not diminish their validity. Researchers who judge treatments using the scientific method are concerned by this viewpoint, since it fails to address the possible inefficacy of alternative treatments.

A major objection to alternative medicine is that it may be done in place of conventional medical treatments. As long as alternative treatments are used alongside conventional treatments, the majority of medical doctors find most forms of complementary medicine acceptable. Consistent with previous studies, the CDC recently reported that the majority of individuals in the United States used CAM in conjunction with conventional medicine.

It is advisable for patients to inform their medical doctor when they are using alternative medicine, because some alternative treatments may interact with orthodox medical treatments, and such potential conflicts should be explored in the interest of the patient. However, many conventional practitioners are biased or uninformed about alternatives, and patients are often reluctant to share this information with their medical doctors since they fear it will hurt their doctor-patient relationship. The issue of alternative medicine interfering with conventional medical practices is minimised when it is turned to only after conventional treatments have been exhausted. Many patients feel that alternative medicine may help in coping with chronic illnesses for which conventional medicine offers no cure, only management. Over time, it has become more common for a patient's own MD to suggest alternatives when they cannot offer effective treatment.

10.4.1. Integrative Medicine

Integrative medicine is a branch of alternative medicine which claims to limit itself to methods with strong scientific evidence of efficacy and safety.

Health geography can provide a spatial understanding of a population's health, the distribution of disease in an area, and the environment's effect on health and disease. It deals also with accessibility to health care and spatial distribution of health care providers. The study is considered a subdiscipline of human geography, however, it requires an understanding of other fields such as epidemiology, climatology.

Although health care is a public good, it is not 'pure'. In other words, it is not equally available to all individuals. The geography of health care provision has much to do with this. Demand for public services is continuously distributed across space, broadly in accordance with the distribution of population, but these services are only provided at discrete locations.

Inevitably therefore, there will be inequalities of access in terms of the practicality of using services, transport costs, travel times and so on. Geographical or 'locational' factors are not the only aspects which influence access to health care. Other types (or dimensions) of accessibility to health care except for geographical (or spatial) are social, financial and functional.

Social accessibility to health care depends on race, age, sex and other social characteristics of individuals, important here is also relationship between patient and the doctor. Financial depends upon the price of a particular health care and functional reflects the amount and structure of provided services. This can vary among different countries or regions of the world. Access to health care is influenced also by factors such as opening times and waiting lists that play an important part in determining whether individuals or population sub-groups can access health care - this type of accessibility is termed 'effective accessibility'.

The location of health care facilities depends largely on the nature of the health care system in operation, and will be heavily influenced by historical factors due to the heavy investment costs in facilities such as hospitals and surgeries. Simple distance will be mediated by organisational factors such as the existence of a referral system by which patients are directed towards particular parts of the hospital sector by their GP. Access to primary care is therefore a very significant component of access to the whole system.

10.5. Conclusion

Everyone has the right to health protection and care. The state guarantees this right by providing free medical and hospital care by means of the installations of the rural medical service network, polyclinics, hospitals, preventative and specialised treatment centers; by providing free dental care; by promoting the health publicity campaigns, health education, regular medical examinations, general vaccinations and other measures to prevent the outbreak of disease. All the population cooperates in these activities and plans through the social and mass organisations.

Health geography is the application of geographical information, perspectives, and methods to the study of health, disease, and health care. Initially referred to as medical geography it was based on the bio-medical model of health and grounded in the logical positivism philosophy. The social or socio-ecological model, adopts a more holistic approach to disease and illness. It emphasises treatment of the whole person and not just components of the system. Under this model, new illnesses (for eg. mental ill health) are recognised, and other types of medicine (for eg. complementary or alternative medicine) are combined with traditional medicine. This alternative methodological approach meant medical geography was broadened to incorporate philosophies such as structuration, structuralism, social interactionism, feminism, et cetera. Thus the field of health geography was born.

References

Akhtar, Rais, *Geography Of Health: An Essay and A Bibliography*, 1982

Clifford, Nicholas and Valentine, Gil, eds., *Key methods in geography*, Suzzallo/Allen Stacks, 2003

Flowerdew, Robin and Martin, David, eds., *Methods in human geography: a guide for students doing research projects*, Suzzallo/Allen Stacks, 1997

Hart, Chris, *Doing a literature review: releasing the social science research imagination*, Suzzallo/Allen Stacks, Tacoma, 1998.

Hay, Iain, ed., *Qualitative research methods in human geography*, Suzzallo/Allen Stacks, 2000

Kearns, Robin A. and Gesler, Wilbert M., *Culture/Place/Health*, Health Sciences Books, Suzzallo/Allen Stacks, 2002.

Kitchin, Rob, *Conducting research in human geography: theory, methodology and practice,* Suzzallo/Allen Stacks, 2000

Lang, Laura, *GIS for health organizations,* Tacoma, 2000

Mackay, Judith, *State Of Health Atlas,* Health Sciences & Soc Work Reference, 1993

Ricketts, Thomas C., et al editors, *Geographic Methods For Health Services Research: A Focus On The Rural- Urban Continuum,* Health Sciences Library, 1994.

Robinson, G. M. (Guy M.), *Methods and techniques in human geography,* Suzzallo/Allen Stacks, 1998

Bibliography

Agnew J., *Political geography: a reader*, London: Arnold, 1997.

Agnew, John, David N. Livingstone, and Alisdair Rogers, eds., *Human Geography: An Essential Anthology*, Oxford and Cambridge, Mass.: Blackwell, 1996.

Aitken, Stuart C., "Public participation, technological discourses and the scale of GIS". In W. Craig, T. Harris, and D. Weiner, eds., *Community Participation and Geographic Information Systems*. Taylor and Francis, 2001.

_____________ .,"Families, communities, and scale of difference", *Social and Cultural Geography* 1(1), 2000.

Akhtar, Rais, *Geography Of Health: An Essay and A Bibliography*, 1982

Alan R.H. Baker and Derek Gregory (eds.), *Explorations in Historical Geography*, 1984.

_____________ and Mark Billinge (eds.), *Period and Place: Research Methods in Historical Geography*, 1982.

Backler, A., & Hanvey R., *Global geography*, NY: Teachers College Press, 1986.

_____________ ., & Stoltman, J., *A teacher's guide to global geography*, Bloomington, IN: Agency for Instructional Technology, 1988.

Berry, Brian J.L., *Comparative Urbanization*, rev. and enl. 2nd ed., 1981.

Bourne L.S., R. Sinclair, and K. Dziewónski (eds.), *Urbanization and Settlement Systems*, 1984.

Buleon P., 'The state of political geography in France in the 1970s and 1980s', *Progress in Human Geography*, Vol. 16 (1), 1992.

Burbank M.J., "The psychological basis of contextual effects", *Political Geography* 14 (6-7), 1995.

Butler, David L., "Technogeopolitics and the struggle for control of world air routes, 1910-1928", *Political Geography* 20 (5), 2001.

Byron J., "Globalization and Neoliberalism: The Caribbean Context", *Political Geography* 18 (7), 1999.

Caesar, Terry, "Motherhood and postmodernism", *American Literary History,* 1995.

Carmines E.G., R. Huckfeldt, C. McCurley, "Mobilization, counter-mobilization and the politics of race", *Political Geography,* 14 (6-7), 1995.

Carter S.K., "The Rise and Fall of State Socialism", *Political Geography,* 17 (8), 1998.

Chan S., "Ethics and International Relations", *Political Geography,* 17 (6), 1998.

Chopra J., "The space of peace-maintenance", *Political Geography,* 15 (3-4), 1996.

Chouinard, Vera, "Structure and agency: Contested concepts in Human Geography", in C. Earle, K. Matthewson, and M.S. Kenzer, eds., *Concepts in Human Geography,* Lanham, MD: Rowman and Littlefield, 1997.

Christiansen T., "Creating Boundaries: The Politics of Race and Nation", *Political Geography,* 17 (8), 1998.

Clark, Michael J., Kenneth J. Gregory, and Angela M. Gurnell, eds., *Horizons in Physical Geography,* Basingstoke and London: Macmillan Education, 1987.

Clifford, Nicholas and Valentine, Gil, eds., *Key methods in geography,* Suzzallo/Allen Stacks, 2003

Cosgrove, Denis, *Apollo's Eye: A Cartographic Genealogy of the Earth in the Western Imagination,* Baltimore and London: John Hopkins University Press, 2001.

Davis, D.R., "Market Access, Economic Geographyand Comparative Advantage: An Empirical Assessment", *Journal of International Economics,* Vol. 2003.

_______________ ., and Weinstein, D.E., "Economic geography and regional production structure: An empirical investigation", *European Economic Review,* Vol. 43, 1999.

Diamond, Jared, *Guns, Germs, and Steel: The Fates of Human Societies,* New York: Norton, 1999.

Dodgshon, R.A. and R.A. Butlin, ed., *An Historical Geography of England and Wales,* second edition, London, 1990.

Entrikin, J. Nicholas, and Stanley D. Brunn, eds. Reflections on Richard Hartshorne's "The Nature of Geography", Washington, D.C.: Association of American Geographers, 1989.

Feenberg A., *"Critical Theory of Technology"*, SFU. 22 May, 2006.

Flowerdew, Robin and Martin, David, eds., *Methods in human geography: a guide for students doing research projects,* Suzzallo/Allen Stacks, 1997

Fujita M., "Urban Economic Theory: Land Use and City Size", Cambridge University Press, 1991.

_______________ ., Henderson J.V., and Mori T.,"Spatial Distribution of Economic Activities in Japan and China", *Handbook of Regional and Urban Economics*, Vol.4. 2004.

Gary A. Goreham, *Encyclopedia of rural America: the land and people,* (editor) Santa Barbara, Calif.: ABC-CLIO, 1997.

Gary L. Peters and Robert P. Larkin, *Population Geography,* 2nd ed. 1983.

George A. Schnell and Mark S. Monmonier, *The Study of Population,* 1983.

Haggett, Peter, *Geography: A Modern Synthesis,* 2nd ed., New York: Harper and Row, 1975.

Harold Carter, *The Study of Urban Geography,* 3rd ed., 1981.

Hart, Chris, *Doing a literature review: releasing the social science research imagination,* Suzzallo/Allen Stacks, Tacoma, 1998.

Hartshorne, Richard, "The Nature of Geography: A Critical Survey of Current Thought in the Light of the Past", Lancaster, Pa.: The Association, 1939.

_______________ , *Perspective on the Nature of Geography,* Chicago: Published by Rand McNally and Company as Monograph No. 1, 1959.

Harvey D., *Justice, nature and the geography of difference,* Oxford: Blackwell, 1996

Harvey, David, *Spaces of the Capital: Towards a Critical Geography,* Edinburgh: Edinburgh University Press, 2001.

Hay, Iain, ed., *Qualitative research methods in human geography,* Suzzallo/Allen Stacks, 2000

Hayes-Bohanan, James, *What is Environmental Geography, Anyway?.* Retrieved on October 9, 2006.

Herbert David T. and Colin J. Thomas, *Urban Geography,* 1982.

Holdsworth D.W., "Historical geography: New ways of imaging and seeing the past", *Progress in Human Geography,* 2003.

_______________ ., "Historical geography: The ancients and the moderns – generational vitality", *Progress in Human Geography,* 2002.

Huw R. Jones, *A Population Geography,* 1981.

Jackson, P., "The cultural politics of masculinity: Towards a social geography", *Transactions, Institute of British Geographers,* 1991.

Jean Gottmann, *Megalopolis: The Urbanized Northeastern Seaboard of the United States,* 1961.

John I. Clarke (ed.), *Geography and Population,* 1984.

Johnston R.J., *Political, electoral and spatial systems,* Oxford: Clarendon Press, 1979

Jordan Terry G. and Lester Rowntree, *The Human Mosaic: A Thematic Introduction to Cultural Geography,* 4th ed., 1986.

Jumper, S.R., "Baccalaureate curricula in geography: Need for consensus guidelines", *Journal of Geography,* 1994.

Kearns, Robin A. and Gesler, Wilbert M., *Culture/Place/Health,* Health Sciences Books, Suzzallo/Allen Stacks, 2002.

Kitchin, Rob, *Conducting research in human geography: theory, methodology and practice,* Suzzallo/Allen Stacks, 2000

Knowles A.K., *Historical Geography,* vol. 33, 2005.

Knox, Paul, *Urban Social Geography: An Introduction,* 2nd ed., 1987.

Lang, Laura, *GIS for health organizations,* Tacoma, 2000

Larkin, Robert P. and Peters, Gary L., *Dictionary of concepts in human geography,* Westport, CT: Greenwood Press, 1983.

Leighly John (ed.), *Land and Life: A Selection from the Writings of Carl Ortwin Sauer,* 1963.

Leszek A. Kosínski and R. Mansell Prothero (eds.), *People on the Move: Studies on Internal Migration,* 1975.

Ley, David, *A Social Geography of the City,* 1983.

Livingston, David N., and Charles W. J. Withers, eds., *Geography and Enlightenment,* Chicago: University of Chicago Press, 1999.

Mackay, Judith, *State Of Health Atlas,* Health Sciences & Soc Work Reference, 1993

Marriott, Alan and Sanchez, John, "The integration of family planning and development activities in India", *Geography,* 1998.

Maurice Yeates and Barry Garner, *The North American City,* 3rd ed., 1980.

McManis, Douglas R., *Historical geography of the United States; a bibliography, excluding Alaska and Hawaii,* Eastern Michigan University, 1965.

Meyer-Arendt, K.J., "Historical Coastal Environmental Changes: Human Response to Shoreline Erosion", in *The American Environment: Interpretations of Past Geographies* (L. Dilsaver & C. Colten, eds.), Savage, MD: Rowman & Littlefield, 1992.

Mittal, P. & Dua, Geeta, *Historical Geography of India,* 2 Vols., 2005

Monkhouse, Francis John, *A dictionary of geography,* 2nd ed. London: Edward Arnold, 1970.

Nordstrom, K.F. and Jackson, N. L., "Temporal and spatial scales of landscape change following storms on human-altered coasts", *Journal of Coastal Conservation*, 1995.

Painter J., *Politics, geography and 'political geography': a critical perspective*, London: Arnold, 1995.

Pattison, W.D., "The Four Traditions of Geography", *Journal of Geography*, 1990.

Pepper D., *Modern environmentalism*, London: Routledge, 1996.

Philip M. Hauser (ed.), *World Population and Development*, 1979.

Phillips, J. D., "Human agency, Holocene sea level, and floodplain accretion in coastal plain rivers", *Journal of Coastal Research*, 1997.

Quaino, Massimo, *Geography and Marxism*, Translated by Alan Braley, Totowa, N.J.: Barnes and Noble, 1982.

Redding S., and A. Venables, "Economic Geography and International Inequality", *Journal of International Economics*, 2004.

Ricketts, Thomas C., et al editors, *Geographic Methods For Health Services Research: A Focus On The Rural- Urban Continuum*, Health Sciences Library, 1994.

Risa Palm, *The Geography of American Cities*, 1981.

Robinson, G. M. (Guy M.), *Methods and techniques in human geography*, Suzzallo/Allen Stacks, 1998

Romm, James S., *The Edges of the Earth in Ancient Thought: Geography, Exploration, and Fiction*, Princeton, N.J.: Princeton University Press, 1992.

Sack R.D., *Human territoriality: its theory and history*, Cambridge: Cambridge University Press, 1986.

Short J.R., *An introduction to political geography*, 2nd edn., London: Routledge, 1993.

Smith, C.T., *An Historical Geography of Western Europe Before 1800*, 1967.

Spencer J.E. and William L. Thomas, *Introducing Cultural Geography*, 2nd ed., 1978.

Stanley D. Brunn and Jack F. Williams (eds.), *Cities of the World: World Regional Urban Development*, 1983.

__________ and James O. Wheeler (eds.), *The American Metropolitan System*, 1980.

Sullivan, Dan, *Mapmaking and its History*, Rutgers University, 2000.

Taylor P.J., *Political geography: world economy, nation state and locality*, Harlow: Longman Scientific & Technical, 1993.

Thomas William L. (ed.), *Man's Role in Changing the Face of the Earth*, 1956, reissued in 2 vol., 1970.

Thrower, Norman J. W., *Maps and Civilization: Cartography in Culture and Society*, 2nd ed. Chicago and London: University of Chicago Press, 1999.

Truman Asa Hartshorn, *Interpreting the City: An Urban Geography*, 1980.

Vallega, A., "Ocean geography vis-à-vis global change and sustainable development", *The Professional Geographer*, 1999.

Wagner Philip L. and Marvin W. Mikesell (eds.), *Readings in Cultural Geography*, 1962.

Walker, H. J., "Nature, humans, and the coastal zone", *The International Journal of Social Education*, 1990.

——————., "The coastal zone", In *The Earth as Transformed by Human Action*, ed. B. L. Turner, Cambridge: Cambridge University Press, 1990.

Ward, Dederick C., Wheeler, Marjorie W. and Bier, Robert A., Jr., *Geologic reference sources: a subject and regional bibliography of publications and maps in the geological sciences*, 2nd ed. Metuchen, NJ: Scarecrow Press, 1981.

Wilbur Zelinsky, Leszek A. Kosínski, and R. Mansell Prothero (eds.), *Geography and a Crowding World*, 1970.

William Norton, *Historical Analysis in Geography*, 1984.

Index